Annamaria Gius

The Baptistery of San Giovanni in Florence

Mandragora

The Baptistery
of San Giovanni
in Florence

A hearty acknowledgement is due to Franco Cosimo Panini Editore, who kindly contributed part of the photographic material used in this guidebook.

La Mandragora s.r.l.
piazza Duomo 9, 50122 Firenze
www.mandragora.it

Captions and glossary: Monica Fintoni

Translated by Steven Grieco

Photographs: Mandragora Archives, Mario Falsini, Mario Ronchetti, Paolo Tosi, Opificio delle Pietre Dure, Archivio Fratelli Alinari

Printed in Italy

ISBN 88-85957-55-2

This book is printed on TCF (totally chlorine free) paper

Contents

Foreword

*Most of the people who have sought
the world over say that this is the loveliest
temple or church to be found anywhere…*
Giovanni Villani, Cronica, II, 23

The Cathedral of Santa Maria del Fiore and the Baptistery of San Giovanni are Florence's two most important religious buildings. While today they are both managed by Opera di Santa Maria del Fiore (Florence Cathedral's vestry board), from the Middle Ages right up to the 18th century they were separate entities, each being run by a different guild.

Indeed, the Republic of Florence founded Opera di Santa Maria del Fiore in 1296 to build the new cathedral, and in 1331 placed it under the patronage of the rich and powerful Arte della Lana (Wool Guild), to speed up construction work. The Baptistery, on the other hand, was always administrated by Arte di Calimala (Merchants' Guild). To this day, Arte della Lana's coat of arms depicting the Agnus Dei serves as an emblem for Opera del Duomo, while the Calimala eagle appears in several locations on the Baptistery's exterior and interior.

In 1770 Peter Leopold of Lorraine, Grand Duke of Tuscany, abolished the Florentine guilds. Seven years later he put the Baptistery under the management of Opera di Santa Maria del Fiore, whose job it was – and still is today – to maintain, refurbish, and enhance both these historic monuments.

The present study traces the history of this baptismal church, describing its superb marble inlays, the magnificent doors cast for its portals by Andrea Pisano and Lorenzo Ghiberti, and the glittering mosaics in its interior narrating the story of humankind from its fall to its redemption. Finally, it surveys the Baptistery's furnishings – masterpieces of sculpture and gold work and priceless historical documents as well – housed today in the nearby Opera del Duomo Museum. An artistic heritage built up over a period spanning ten centuries, thanks to the enormous financial, intellectual and artistic resources that were focussed on this seat of Florence's religious life.

Anna Mitrano
*Head of the Opera
di Santa Maria del Fiore*

I. The Baptistery and the City

A Monument and a Symbol

In many views of Florence dating from the 14th and 15th centuries the Baptistery stands out as the most prominent monument, unmistakable in its sheathing of pure white marble neatly inlaid with geometric patterns in green serpentine stone of Prato. This is no coincidence. Right beside the Baptistery stood the unfinished but ornate façade of Santa Maria del Fiore, designed by Arnolfo di Cambio at the end of the 13th century, and Giotto's soaring Campanile. Then, after 1438, came Brunelleschi's superb pavilion-shaped cupola, built high enough to be visible far beyond the city's actual boundaries, "so that it may extend its shadow over all the peoples of Tuscany", said Leon Battista Alberti with a striking hyperbole. But for all Florentines, the Baptistery remained their city's chief monument and symbol. A good deal older than the buildings surrounding it – so ancient, indeed, that its beginnings were shrouded in legend – the Baptistery best expressed the people's religious, civic and artistic identity.

Always caustic about the city that had cast him out, Dante Alighieri nevertheless described the Baptistery in sober but nostalgic tones: "my lovely San Giovanni". The building was linked in his memory with a vivid picture of how he had once rushed to save a new-born child that had fallen into the baptismal font.

For many centuries the Baptistery was the temple in which all men and women were initiated into the Christian faith, the place where the sacrament of baptism blazed a path to Paradise lost and wiped out the taint of original sin. By 313 AD, the year in which Constantine issued his Edict granting freedom of worship to all Christians, the new religion had already taken root in Florence. In these early times, baptism was administered to adult individuals rather than to infants, and celebrated on the Saturday night preceding Easter Sunday. The rite provided for the individual's full immersion in the font, in remembrance of how St John had baptized Jesus Christ on the banks of the River Jordan.

Plans for a proper building in which to celebrate this most basic of Christian sacraments got underway in 394, when St Ambrose, Bishop of Milan, came to consecrate Florence's first basilica, San Lorenzo. Even in later times, after the cathedral was completed (and subsequently enlarged), the Baptistery never ceased to be the city's religious core. It was for this reason, perhaps, that its origins were enveloped in legend. Giovanni Villani's 14th-century *Cronica* cites the popular belief that the Baptistery had originally been "a wonderful temple in honour of the God

Opposite page: the Baptistery, seen from the top of the Campanile di Giotto. This baptismal church is dedicated to St John the Baptist, Florence's patron Saint. In the Middle Ages it came to have a civic and political significance that ran parallel to its crucial religious function. In medieval chronicles in particular the building became endowed with a legendary quality.

Mars", whose equestrian monument allegedly stood atop a column at the centre of the temple. This credence was so firmly entrenched in the people of Florence that it survived till the early 1900s. The temple was thought to have been built under the Emperor Augustus, to celebrate the Romans' successful subjugation of the Etruscan Fiesole. Villani's account later became the subject of a striking panel painting, the *Founding of Florence*, which Giorgio Vasari did in 1563 for the ceiling of Palazzo Vecchio's Sala dei Cinquecento. In the background we see an octagonal temple open at the top and on all sides – clearly the Baptistery in Roman garb – with an equestrian statue at its centre.

In the newly prosperous city-states of Medieval and Renaissance Tuscany, it was common practice to claim noble origins by tracing one's ancestry back to ancient Rome. If the Pisans, a seafaring people looking both to East and West, imagined their city to have been founded by Aeneas after his escape from Troy, let us not be surprised if the more bellicose Florence should link the earliest history of its chief monument to

This scene from the "Biadaiolo" Manuscript (Florence, Biblioteca Medicea Laurenziana, Tempi 3, c. 58 r) records an episode that took place during the famine that hit Tuscany between 1328 and 1330. A group of paupers expelled from the town of Siena reach the doors of Florence, where they are given assistance. The segments of the Baptistery roof – visible on the right, with the Bargello tower in the background – are marked by projecting ribs. These were removed during the restoration program of 1898-1908. The placing of the stairway leading up to the lantern on the south side is fictional, for in those times it was on the east side of the roof. The manuscript (ca. 1344-1347) derives its name from the profession of its owner, Domenico Lenzi, a "biadaiolo", or corn-merchant. Here he entered not only the prices of grains he put on the market of Orsanmichele, but also added verses, miscellaneous information and moralistic maxims.

Augustus' victory over the enemy. Although this belief has since been put to rest, 19th-century excavations did nevertheless bring to light the remains of a 3rd century Roman construction beneath the present Baptistery. Its pre-Medieval beginnings, almost unanimously denied by 20th-century scholars, have received fresh support from recent research, which tentatively places the building's foundations around the late 4th or early 5th centuries AD, at a time when the declining Roman Empire was passing on its vast heritage of art forms to the rising Christian civilization. This appears to be further substantiated by the fact that the excavations beneath the Baptistery have not yielded Roman coins dating later than the early 5th century.

Giorgio Vasari, The Founding of Florentia, *detail (ceiling of the Salone dei Cinquecento, Palazzo Vecchio, Florence). The origins of the Baptistery have been the subject of lively debate for centuries. Up to the mid 16th century it was generally believed to be a Roman temple of Mars (Florence's "first master" according to Dante), dating from late antiquity or even from the time of Augustus, with the statue of this Roman war god standing in the place of the baptismal font. Vasari faithfully rendered this tradition, based on the "chronicles of old", in his imaginary reconstruction of 1563. The building is conceived as a sort of eight-sided pavilion; at its centre is the equestrian statue of Mars on top of a tall column. It is not clear whether Vasari intended this to be considered a primitive version of the Baptistery. But there is no doubt that in his attempt to establish a continuity with the Roman world Vasari conceived his fresco as a hardly disguised celebration of the Medici family, worthy heirs of the Caesars. These implications were not lost upon his contemporaries, and indeed fuelled a heated controversy between Vincenzo Borghini, a Benedictine scholar-monk who championed the pro-Medici theory of the building's Roman origins (probably also directly inspiring Vasari's work), and Gerolamo Mei, an erudite antiquarian who strongly opposed this theory.*

The "Lovely San Giovanni" during the Middle Ages

There is no doubt that the present appearance of the Baptistery, with its exterior inlays of green and white marble, is the medieval version of an earlier building.

The oldest mention of a Baptistery building – rising in this spot, halfway between the Bishop's Residence and the Cathedral – goes back to the year 897. In 1059, a year after he stepped down as Bishop of Florence, Pope Nicholas II consecrated the building a second time. Some authorities consider this to be the true founding date of the Baptistery, such as it has come down to us. It is only in the 12th century, as Florentine history grew more eventful and therefore more memorable, that further reliable information becomes available. As the city struggled to gain supremacy over its neighbours, the Baptistery soon became the chief monument and symbol of Florence, an inheritance which ancient Rome had bequeathed to the city, urging it to accomplish deeds as great as its own. The building was appointed to house the insignia of Florence and of the towns subject to it, as well as the trophies wrested from the enemy after victorious battles. In 1487 these historic objects were removed from the Baptistery, and it was forbidden to hang cloths or any other objects on its walls – clearly a sign that the city's cultural atmosphere had become more sensitive to artistic values than to the civic memories of its recent past. The only exception was two porphyry columns standing on either side of the Gates of Paradise. This was a gift from Pisa to Florence, to commemorate a joint victory over the Moors of the Balearic Islands in the naval battle of 1117. The war cry "Saint John!" – which the Florentine armies uttered before entering the fray – may well have resounded on that occasion, too.

The growing importance of the Baptistery as a temple glorifying the city's history in no way overshadowed its religious significance. This aspect was clearly underlined in the early 1200s, with the construction of the monumental marble baptismal font to celebrate the rite of full immersion, which at that time was still practised. The light entering from the recently constructed lantern crowning the dome fell on the great octagonal basin, and was a literal illustration of the 'enlightenment' which baptism brings to man. Excavations have shown that in the area between the octagonal baptismal font and the rectangular apse there stood a smaller basin in which, according to the Ambrosian rite, the newly baptized had their feet washed immediately after baptism.

Workshop of Bernardo Daddi, Madonna of Mercy, *detail (Sala del Capitano, Confraternita del Bigallo, Florence). In this fresco, at the feet of a hieratic Madonna surrounded by the faithful, we see one of the best known representations of Florence in the Middle Ages (mid 14th century). The Campanile di Giotto is still under construction (completed 1359), while the façade of the Cathedral appears in its first sheathing of polychrome marbles and mosaics (removed at the end of the 16th century). The Baptistery is depicted as being much bigger – exaggeratedly so – than the buildings surrounding it. This is a clear demonstration of this monument's vital importance to all Florentines in the Middle Ages as a symbol of their city's civil and political unity.*

A Burial Place

As the Baptistery had welcomed them at birth, so Florentines cherished the idea that they would end their earthly existence in this place and from here reach everlasting life. Even though burial inside the Baptistery was a rare privilege indeed, there was a vast burial ground surrounding the building, which had probably been in use ever since the 6th century AD. Giovanni Villani notes that the nearby Guardamorto tower was thus named because "in the olden times all good folk who died were buried at San Giovanni". The tower was torn down in 1248, during the civil strife between Guelfs and Ghibellines. At about the same time, Boccaccio writes that the poet Guido Cavalcanti eluded some individuals who were pestering him by fleeing amidst "the great marble coffins, which today are in Santa Reparata, and many others all around San Giovanni". In the 12th century deceased members of patrician families in Florence, Pisa and Lucca were often buried in ancient or medieval sarcophagi. Two such stone coffins reused in medieval times can be seen today inside the Baptistery (see p. 55), whilst others are in the nearby Opera del Duomo Museum. By the end of the 13th century the sarcophagi lying close to the Baptistery's outside walls were gradually removed to complete the building's outer marble panelling and to turn the surrounding area into a more spacious concourse. This was probably why in the late 1300s the hoary practice of interring the members of prominent families in the open square between the Baptistery and the Cathedral was stopped. Evidence of this came to light during excavations made in the 19th century and in the 1960s. Such graves consisted of rectangular-shaped trenches, dug in close proximity to each other, and sealed with inscribed tombstones which probably also served as flagstones to cover the square.

St John's Day Celebrations

The open ground surrounding the Baptistery was eventually reserved for celebrations honouring the city's patron Saint. These became increasingly important throughout the Middle Ages.

St John's Day was first celebrated in Florence in 1084. Two centuries later this feast had grown into a major event. For three days all daily business in the city came to a halt, as its inhabitants funneled all their energies into celebrating a holiday which was not only religious, but political, civic and military as well. Florence would don its holiday attire in good time. The doors and windows of all houses were decorated with festive cloths. Rugs were rolled out in the streets and squares, while shops put on show their most prized goods. On the morning of June 23rd, St John's Eve, the city's clergy and its monastic orders walked in solemn procession to the open space between the Baptistery and the Cathedral. The ground had been covered with a large blue canvas cloth decorated with golden lilies. It was here that, from the 14th century on, the silver altar of St John the Baptist (see p. 116) was displayed to the crowds, laden with a sumptuous array of sacred objects. In the evening the citizens offered up large votive candles to their patron Saint. On St John's Day the Saint was presented with more costly gifts, which also came from the territories under Florentine rule. The representatives of the vassal towns first rendered homage to the city elders in Palazzo Vecchio, and then proceeded to the Baptistery carrying their candles. After the mid-1300s, these candles blossomed into small wooden or papier-maché towers, hollowed out so as to fit one or more bearers inside. After reaching the Baptistery, they were lined up along the building's interior walls, where they stood for the next twelve months. In the afternoon, the different city quarters competed in a horse race, in the presence of a cheering crowd. The scene must not have been very different from today's Palio di Siena, with the excitement running to red-hot levels. The horse race marked the end of the three-day-long festivities.

In the 15th century the secular aspects of the feast took on more prominence, thanks to the procession of the *edifizi*, held on June 22nd. These were cars on which actors staged dramatic scenes. By Lorenzo the Magnificent's time, the *edifizi* had come to be very much like the allegorical or mythological *trionfi*, used during Carnival time and for other profane events. After the brief expulsion of the Medici from Florence, Savonarola's austere Republic forbade the festivities marking St John's Day. They were promptly resumed upon the Medici's return to

Below: the front panel of a wedding chest dating from the 1430s. Attributed to Giovanni Toscani, it portrays The Procession of the Banners (Bargello Museum, Florence). St John's Day falls on the 24th of June, and in the past in Florence this feast was marked by a wealth of celebrations. The inhabitants of the surrounding countryside came to the city to offer large tapers to the Saint. Their gifts not only had a devotional meaning, but were also a tangible tribute to Florence's political primacy over the towns subject to it. The offering of the "palii" was equally important. These were large banners of painted cloth, which were used to decorate the walls in the Baptistery's interior. On the front panel of the chest we see a sumptuous procession on horseback escorting the gift. The Baptistery building is seen from the south side, and its south portal is still surmounted by Tino di Camaino's sculptural group depicting the Baptism of Christ. Only the bust of the Christ raising his hand in blessing has survived. It was found in 1844 in the courtyard of the priest's residence. Today it is at the Opera del Duomo Museum (→ pp. 116-117).

Girolamo Savonarola at the Stake, panel painting attributed to Francesco Roselli, a painter and contemporary of the Ferrara-born preacher (Museum of San Marco, Florence). After the expulsion of the Medici from Florence in 1494 this puritanical Dominican monk stopped the festive celebrations marking St John's Day, on the grounds that they had become blatantly profane over the years. After the Medici family's return to Florence, the processions once again became popular. The later grand dukes of the Habsburg-Lorraine dynasty allowed them to continue, albeit with less fanfare.

power. After Florence lost its status as a free city and came under the heel of the Medici, the civil and political significance of these celebrations tended to disappear. They were replaced by a feast that was both religious and secular, held with the pomp and pageantry which became the hallmark of so many public events under Medici rule. In 1655 Ferdinando II ordered the construction of St John's Chair. This ceremonial seat was covered in gold and silver, while the back was draped with an embroidered, jewel-studded cloth depicting St John in the wilderness. Towards the end of the procession, the Grand Duke seated himself in this chair and received the tribute which the subject towns and the nobility offered him – usually an array of precious objects, money and even food. Cardinal Lazzaro Pallavicini made one of the most munificent bequests: for 58 consecutive years, till the death of Gian Gastone, last of the Medici rulers, a large silver bowl decorated with figures in relief was offered every year on his behalf. This precious series was melted down during Napoleon's occupation of Tuscany. All that remains to us are the plaster casts, now on show at Museo degli Argenti.

In our present age St John's Day is once again a primarily religious festivity, solemnly celebrated by the clergy and – somewhat less enthusiastically – by the people themselves. On the 24th of June, which still today is a city holiday, Florentines prefer to leave their town in the hands of the ever-growing numbers of tourists. But they do gather in the evening to watch the firework display, perhaps the last memory of the popular acclaim with which this holiday was once greeted. In the 15th century the lighting of bonfires to signify joy and good luck became a widespread practice in all of Tuscany. Fire was seen as a purifying force, eminently capable of honouring St John the Baptist, who had used water to carry out the purification of baptism. Perhaps even our disenchanted contemporaries, as they lift their gaze to the night sky brightly lit by colourful fireworks, try to find in this worldly event a reminder of a centuries-old trust in their patron Saint's promise of protection and salvation.

II. The Baptistery Over the Centuries

Controversy Over Its Origins

However much it has been studied and extolled, the Baptistery continues to put students of architecture at odds over the crucial question of its founding date. We have seen that in the past the building was believed to be a Christian adaptation of an Augustan temple of Mars (see pp. 9-11). We know now that its walls do indeed rest on the foundations of Roman buildings dating from the 1st and 3rd centuries AD. 19th-century excavations conclusively established this fact, thus putting to rest that intriguing legend, which had been nevertheless discredited by scholars as early as the 17th century. On the other hand, the building's undeniably classical structure – which it owes more to its ground plan and proportions than to its outer cloak of marble – has convinced many authorities that the Baptistery can be dated back to the early Christian centuries, and that its architecture is still directly influenced by ancient Roman models; the marble inlays being added between the 11th and 12th centuries, in harmony with the decorative canons of the Tuscan High Romanesque. Others believe that the build-

The 1898-1908 excavations under the Baptistery unearthed the floor levels of Roman dwellings dating from the 1st to the 3rd centuries AD. Underneath the apse in particular, are parts of floor mosaics decorated with simple geometrical patterns which are still visible today. These findings fuelled different theories regarding the settlements existing in this spot prior to the construction of the Baptistery, and have all but definitively invalidated the theory that the building has classical origins.

ing and its marble decoration are both part of a continuous construction process occurring throughout the high Middle Ages and inspired by a conscious revival of ancient Roman architectural forms.

Documents from 897 AD to the year 1000 mention an "ecclesia", or church, of San Giovanni standing in front of the Bishop's Palace, but excavations underneath the present building have yielded no evidence of this. The restructuring of an older building – or perhaps the construction of a brand new one – is linked to Pope Nicholas II, who consecrated the Baptistery on November 6, 1059. Those who believe the Baptistery to have been founded in the Middle Ages take this date to mark the beginning of construction work. They also assume that by the early years of the 1100s at least a part of the green and white marble panelling of the exterior had been completed, thus inspiring the decorative scheme on the tomb of Bishop Ranieri (died 1113) inside the Baptistery (see p. 57).

Construction of the Baptistery

In 1128 the baptismal font was moved from Santa Reparata to the Baptistery. The two churches stand opposite each other, and christenings were probably celebrated in the former while San Giovanni was under construction. It is safe to assume that by that date the Baptistery was in good functioning order and probably already equipped with its dome. An unsupported tradition – once again influenced by the structure's classical appearance – has it that the dome originally had an *oculus*, or large opening at its summit, like the Pantheon in Rome. Towards the middle of the 12th century Arte di Calimala, the Florentine merchants' guild, commissioned the lantern that closes and crowns the dome: its purpose was to allow the daylight to play over the dome's concave interior and float downwards gently and solemnly. This is the first instance known to us of this powerful guild financing decorative work for the Baptistery. Over the centuries, Arte di Calimala became a major sponsor of many of the best projects undertaken to beautify the Baptistery. Their object was to make San Giovanni into Florence's chief monument and a symbol of the city's artistic excellence. Like all sponsors worthy of this name, the Arte di Calimala made publicity for itself by having its emblem – an eagle clawing a *torsello*, or bale of wool – carved in several places on the Baptistery, especially on its exterior walls.

A new and memorable phase in the architectural history of the Baptistery began in or around 1202, when the present rectangular apse, or *scarsella*, was built, perhaps in the place of the previous semi-circular structure. Shortly thereafter, the new presbytery was embellished with fine marble furnishings. The monumental altar, which also stood here, was demolished in the Baroque Age and many of its parts were subsequently lost. Drawing inspiration from the 1207 floor mosaic in the nave of San Miniato al Monte, the city replaced the Baptistery's floor of crushed brick (*opus signinum*) with a pattern of marble inlays designed to look like a spread of superb Oriental carpets. This showed the way to the centre of the building, where the great baptismal font mentioned by Dante stood inside a spacious octagonal enclosure. The font was dismantled in 1577, for the solemn christening ceremony of Grand Duke Francesco de' Medici's first born son, amidst the disapproval of those Florentines who were attached to this old and cherished object. The decision was dictated by a typical Renaissance fondness for vast, unbroken spaces, and probably made easier by the fact that the original baptismal font, designed for the rite by immersion, had been superseded by a 14th-century font shaped like a polygonal basin. The latter can still be seen today standing against the south-east wall.

Towards the mid 1200s, while the liturgical and artistic decoration of the ground floor was being completed, work also began on the new decorative scheme for the in-

Opposite page: the Cathedral seen from the building at the corner between Via Cerretani and Piazza San Giovanni. In the foreground, at the bottom, is the column of St Zenobius, which commemorates a miracle connected with this saint. While the body of the deceased bishop was being carried from the nearby church of San Lorenzo to the Cathedral of Santa Reparata (in those days the Cathedral of Florence), an old withered elm tree in the square suddenly burst into blossom. The same tree later supplied the wood panel upon which the late 13th century Master of Bigallo portrayed St Zenobius and the deacons Eugene and Crescentius, today at the Opera del Duomo Museum. Below: the church of San Miniato al Monte. San Miniato and the Baptistery are both typical examples of Florentine Romanesque architecture, which selects architectural elements drawn from Classical and Early Christian antiquity, Byzantine art and the Po Valley and Pisan Romanesque styles, and blends them into a new and deeply original language. It flourished throughout the 11th century. Marble inlay decoration is one of its distinguishing features.

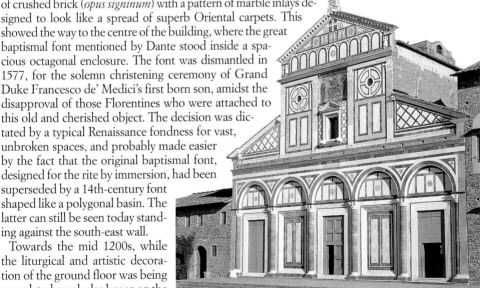

The aedicule containing the copy of the marble group depicting the Baptism of Christ on the east façade of the Baptistery rests on two pedestals decorated with the coat-of-arms of Arte di Calimala, a powerful merchants' guild which held the patronage of the Baptistery for many centuries. Its emblem shows an eagle clawing a "torsello". According to one of the many etymologies offered for this name, Calimala derives from "Calle Maior", the southern stretch of the "cardo", or main street which cuts across the Roman Florence on a north-south axis. Here were located the warehouses of the city's cloth merchants, who in the 13th century purchased rough cloth in Flanders and then processed it into fine fabrics which they exported. Arte di Calimala thus became the richest and most influential of Florence's Arti Maggiori, or major guilds, and for this reason subsidized popular festivals, public works and charity institutions. Throughout the 1200s the guild's political clout was modest, but this state of affairs changed dramatically in 1293, when Giano della Bella's Statutes of Justice laid down that all candidates for the post of city magistrate must join a profession and renounce their noble status.

terior. This included painting the areas in the women's gallery in white and green patterns, in imitation of the marble inlays on the exterior. More significantly, the ambitious job of covering the interior of the dome with mosaics got underway around 1225. The launching of the scheme is recorded in an inscription in the *scarsella*. Thanks to the joint efforts of a great number of painters and mosaicists, this decorative scheme was completed about 80 years later, and can indeed be said to mark one of the crucial stages in the development of the Florentine school of painting. While in the early stages of decorating the dome the city's artists were quite innocent of the complexities of mosaic setting, as work progressed, all of them – including Giotto himself – were able to demonstrate that they had mastered this art as well.

As the mosaics of the dome were nearing completion, their success convinced the authorities to extend them to other areas inside the building, such as the drum of the dome and the parapets in the women's gallery. Both areas were encased in marble panelling, which in the 14th century was covered with brightly coloured glass mosaics. The women's gallery also underwent partial alteration. The sections above the portals were mosaicked, to underscore the symbolic importance of doorways in a temple devoted to baptism. Lippo di Bienivieni, a disciple of Giotto's, was commissioned to paint a tabernacle for the high altar: although this was lost in the wake of later decorative programs, Boccaccio has left us a lively description of it in one of his stories.

In the late 1200s, while the interior of the Baptistery was being completed, the area surrounding the building also underwent transformation. In 1288 the city commissioned Arnolfo di Cambio to "repair, raise and level off the square around the temple of St John the Baptist, and pave it with bricks", in the words of the Latin document detailing the assignment. This celebrated artist designed a fine pavement with a herring-bone pattern of bricks set edgewise. According to Vasari, in 1293 Arnolfo replaced the earlier stone pilasters, which stood at the corners of the façade, with the black and white striped ones we see today.

The architectural details having been completed by the early 14th century (giving the Baptistery roughly the appearance it has today), the merchants of Calimala launched additional projects to decorate the exterior. First came the statuary above the three portals, sculpted by the Sienese artist Tino di Camaino around 1320. This was followed by a project for a set of gilt bronze doors for the main portal facing the cathedral. Andrea Pisano took on the task in 1322, and completed his superb oeuvre in 1366.

As everyday life and business returned to normal after the devastating plague of 1348, work began on an altar embellished with precious silver and enamel ornaments. At first designed as an antependium hanging before the high altar during solemn functions, in the 15th century this grew into a full-fledged altar which was displayed at the centre of the Baptistery – and on certain occasions outside the building as well – laden with all the precious gold objects from the burgeoning Baptistery Treasure.

In the early years of the 15th century – a century that was to mark the high point of Florentine art – Lorenzo Ghiberti won a competition amongst Florence's best goldsmiths and sculptors for a second pair of bronze doors for the Baptistery, and completed them between 1403 and 1424. Shortly thereafter, the authorities commissioned Ghiberti to do the third and last set of doors, the so-called Gates of Paradise, which in 1452 replaced the older doors by Andrea Pisano for the main portal. Meanwhile, another great sculptor, Donatello, made further contributions inside the Baptistery. This included the monumental tomb of Cardinal Baldassarre Cossa, and the dramatic wooden image of *Mary Magdalen*, which was damaged during the 1966 flood, and later placed in the Opera del Duomo Museum (see p. 115).

The construction of the lantern was the first addition to the Baptistery to be financed by Arte di Calimala. According to Giovanni Villani's "Cronica", it was completed in 1150. Topped by a golden globe and a cross, the marble-sheathed lantern closes the building's pyramid-shaped roof, which according to tradition used to be open in the centre like the Pantheon in Rome.

Alterations, Destructions and Restoration Programs

Very soon after their completion, the mosaics on the dome showed signs of deterioration due to rainwater entering through the Baptistery's marble panelled roof. Indeed, the roof had undergone a first overhauling as early as the second half of the 14th century. The gaps in the mosaics had to be filled, and further portions prevented from falling down. For this purpose, the painter Alessio Baldovinetti – one of the last artists in Florence to be acquainted with the technique of setting wall mosaics – was given a permanent assignment in the late 15th century to oversee the refurbishing and upkeep of the mosaics in the Baptistery.

In spite of its reverence for these masterworks of the olden times, which it considered precious incunabula to be bequeathed to later generations, the Renaissance had little appreciation for the other artistic accomplishments of the Middle Ages. The 14th-century statues above the three Baptistery portals were

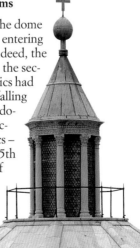

removed from their location during the 1500s, and replaced with the marble *Baptism of Christ*, which Andrea Sansovino carved for the main entrance, and with Giovan Francesco Rustici's and Vincenzo Danti's two bronze groups for the other two doors. The 1577 dismantling of the great baptismal font has already been mentioned (see p. 17). In this case the authorities did not even have the good sense to replace it with a fitting substitute, but instead commissioned Bernardo Buontalenti to design one of those ephemeral décors which the theatrical taste of the Mannerist period so delighted in.

We know precious little about possible alterations carried out in the 17th century. But most probably little was done beyond refurbishing the old and much revered Crucifix altar, located on the right of the main entrance. A more substantial project was launched in 1732 to build a new high altar decorated with polychrome marble panelling and a balustrade, to replace the original Romanesque altar (see p. 56). It was surmounted by Girolamo Ticciati's rather theatrical sculpture, *St John the Baptist in Glory*.

Vast restoration programs of the interior were undertaken in later years. In 1782 the central section of the floor, where the baptismal font had stood in earlier times, was occupied by an octagon decorated with white, red and green geometrical patterns. Two little known painters overhauled the mosaics, and filled the gaps with painted plaster to match the missing portions (see page 109). A third artist restored the mosaics of the dome in 1820-1823, at a time when mosaic setting had become a forgotten art in Florence. This was why the Grand Duke repeatedly urged that for this job mosaicists be sought in Rome, where the technique was still practised.

This photograph taken before the early-20th-century restructuring shows the "scarsella", or rectangular apse, still containing a baroque altar (1730-1732) surmounted by Girolamo Ticciati's sculpture St John the Baptist in Glory *(below), and the octagon decorated with white, red and green geometrical patterns visible in the centre of the floor, now at the Opera del Duomo Museum.*

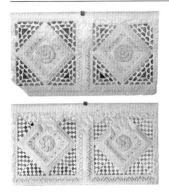

Further renovation programs came in the late 1800s. Excavations begun in 1894 brought to light the lower floor-levels dating from Roman times, as well as medieval tombs in the square outside the Baptistery. Two years later the architect Luigi del Moro worked extensively on the lantern crowning the dome and on its exterior panelling, in an effort to stop the infiltration of rainwater which in past centuries had dealt repeated blows to the mosaics. The prominent ribs running down the edges of the pyramid-shaped roof exterior were also removed. This is how the roof came to have the smooth appearance it has today.

In 1898, after the roof had been waterproofed, Opificio delle Pietre Dure ('Workshop of Semi-precious Stones') started working on the mosaics of the dome and the rectangular apse. The workshop had only recently ceased producing art objects and turned into a laboratory specializing in conservation. For this difficult program, which was carried out in record time and completed by 1907, its restorers perfected a modern technique to detach and reset the crumbling portions of mosaic. They also replaced with new tesserae the gaps which in earlier times had been filled with painted plaster. In keeping with the taste of the times, no effort was spared to make the restored portions resemble the original work. This included a close study of the sinopias, or underdrawings, where these still existed. The work was done so painstakingly that it is not always easy today to make out what portions of the mosaics were redone by the Opificio. A short time later, the architect Giuseppe Castellucci adopted similar principles for his restoration efforts. He removed

Above, left: surviving parts of the 13th century baptismal font (Opera del Duomo Museum, Florence). Mentioned by Dante in a famous and controversial passage of the Divine Comedy, this time-honoured font was demolished in 1577.
Above: a fragment of the sculptural works removed in the 16th century from the Baptistery's exterior walls. Many scholars believe this to be the head of the figure of St John the Baptist that stood between the Levite and the Pharisee above the north portal. The work, which was replaced in 1511 by Giovan Francesco Rustici's bronze group, has been attributed to an artist in the entourage of Tino di Camaino, or Andrea Pisano, and is also now at the Opera del Duomo Museum.
Below, left: the trial reliefs with which Lorenzo Ghiberti and Filippo Brunelleschi competed in the 1401 contest for a second pair of bronze doors for the Baptistery. The subject given was the Sacrifice of Isaac, because at first the Calimala merchants had wanted the panels on the doors to narrate stories from the Old Testament. The trial reliefs submitted by other candidates – every one of them "beautiful and different from the others", according to Vasari – have been lost. Brunelleschi presented his relief (right) to Cosimo the Elder, who put it in the Old Sacristy of the church of San Lorenzo. From here it was moved, together with Ghiberti's, to the Bargello Museum.

In 1990 the original Gates of Paradise were replaced with a bronze replica, sponsored by Tokyo's Sun Motoyama Group. Ghiberti's celebrated masterpiece, which had already been badly damaged by the 1966 Flood, was moved to the laboratory in the Opificio delle Pietre Dure. The doors are presently undergoing lengthy and delicate restoring.

the Baroque altars, including the high altar. This he replaced with the present high altar, whose structure includes a number of original Romanesque parts. He also dismantled the 18th-century octagon in the centre of the Baptistery (now housed at Opera del Duomo Museum), and paved this section of the floor with crushed earthenware, which was intentionally left undistinguished. Finally, he tried to reconstruct the great baptismal font, but never completed it.

After the 1950s, all attempts at a historically faithful type of restoration (typical of the 19th century) were abandoned. Experts now concentrated on the pure and simple conservation of the building, whose exterior was and still is threatened by increasingly aggressive air pollution. In view of this, a difficult – though not final – decision was made to move the most endangered works of art to Opera del Duomo: among them, the Gates of Paradise. Replaced with a copy in 1990, Ghiberti's doors are undergoing laborious restoration to this day.

III. Exterior

The Architectural Plan

General Features

The Baptistery of San Giovanni and the church of San Miniato are both typical examples of the Florentine Romanesque, a noble style that selects and reorganizes architectural elements borrowed from Classical, Early Christian and Byzantine models, as well as from Pisan and Lombard Romanesque buildings. Its remarkable originality, clarity and classical sense of restraint seem to foreshadow the Renaissance. The style flourished in Florence and in its territory during the 11th century, and one of its distinctive features here is the use of decorative marble inlays. While in contemporary Pisan architecture – and in Pisan-influenced Tuscan architecture – marble panelling had a primarily decorative and pictorial function, in Florence it became closely linked to an overall architectural conception that was supremely clear and rational.

This is how the Baptistery appears to us today, with its straightforward octagonal plant, and the tripartite division of each side. While the first two registers match the unfolding of the interior, the third register is an attic storey which masks the impost of the dome. This has pointed arches on the inside and is covered outside by a pitched roof. The division of each of the three registers is likewise threefold. The lower level is divided into sections by pilasters of green marble with foliated capitals. Directly above these stand the polygonal columns of the second, or upper, level, which support three blind arcades. The

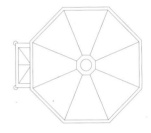

Far from being a casual arrangement, the Baptistery's octagonal floor plan has a precise religious meaning. In his "Exposition of the Gospel According to St Luke" Ambrose states that the number 8 symbolizes the day of the resurrection coming after a Christian's time on earth ("octava enim die facta est resurrectio"), while in the moment the faithful receives baptism he takes his first crucial step on the path leading to redemption.

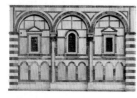

The geometric patterns decorating the three levels of the Baptistery's east wall follow ancient Roman models and were inlaid with green serpentine stone from Prato and white marble from the Carrara quarries (above: the east wall after the restoration program completed in 1993). The corner pilasters, with horizontal black and white stripes on the lower level, are of later execution. In earlier times they were made of plain pietra serena (pale grey Tuscan sandstone). According to Vasari, Arnolfo di Cambio fashioned them in 1293, while working on the new pavement for the Baptistery square. Right: the four-sided rectangular apse built in 1202 to replace the earlier semi-circular one.

green-and-white marble panelling is recessed. Its sober geometrical design perfectly matches the architectural design and echoes its geometrical division of space.

On the second level the marble inlays outline in stylized fashion a small loggia, an abstract version of similar relief designs typical of the Lombard Romanesque. These are an external projection, as it were, of the women's gallery running inside the building. Above the *loggetta* – and perfectly centred below each arch – are alternating pedimented and round-headed windows. Of classical design, their plastic form is modulated in a gentle but definite manner. On the third, or top, register – thought by many to belong to a later period – the strong relief design of the lower levels is simplified, with fluted pilaster strips framing rectangular panels in groups of three. Above these runs a fascia with decorative diamond-shaped and braided inlays.

The 'Scarsella', or Rectangular Apse

The *scarsella*, or rectangular apse, occupies the west side of the Baptistery, and is on the same axis as the building's main entrance. Its exterior – facing the Archbishop's Residence – projects beyond the building's outer contour. Work on the *scarsella* was begun in the early 1200s. As we have already seen, many scholars believe that it replaced an earlier, semi-circular apse. Recent studies have ascertained, however, that the weight of the dome is partly supported by the *scarsella*, a fact that would indicate that the structure is earlier than the dome.

The *scarsella*'s outer marble panelling follows the general scheme of the other decoration on the exterior of the Baptistery. In particular, the addition of a fascia of minute inlays recalls that of the third register. The apse is remarkable for having the only two relief figures to be

seen anywhere on the building. These are the marble angle spouts, or gargoyles, at both corners of the roof, in the shape of half-lions grasping a large human head in their claws. This is an iconographic motif typical of Romanesque sculpture. The two human heads, though heavily disfigured by the elements, appear to be Medieval, while the two lions and the moulded pedestal overhead – especially the right-hand portion as you face the apse – are in such good condition that they could well be a 19th-century reconstruction.

A further sculptural element on the *scarsella* is the lid of what was probably a late Roman sarcophagus, portraying seafaring and grape harvest scenes. It is encased at the foot of the apse's southern wall, and may have served to mark the place of a medieval tomb. Other such marble slabs with burial inscriptions are found at ground level along the Baptistery's outer walls.

The Dome and the Lantern

Stout angle pilasters stand at the corners of the apse and at each corner of the Baptistery's eight sides. According to Vasari, these were hewn out of "macigno" (sandstone). At the end of the 13th century the pilasters were sheathed in stripes of green and white marble, in keeping with the decorative canons typical of western Tuscany in that century.

The main reason for the Baptistery's exterior decoration was to make the building look as if it was wholly made of marble. For this same reason, also the pyramid-shaped roof is, rather unusually, panelled with slabs of white marble, and crowned with a marble lantern which according to the 14th-century chronicler Giovanni Villani was made in the mid 1100s. The date 1174 recorded at the foot of the structure may have been added during the 1898-1907 renovation program. At that time the lantern was disassembled and some of its parts perhaps replaced. Eight slender un-grooved Corinthian colonnettes with foliated capitals support another entablature with three fascias. The plants in low relief on the two outer strips close in the geometrical patterns of the central band. On this entablature rests the lantern's cone-shaped pinnacle – a further development of the geometrical theme lying at the core of the Baptistery's architectural conception. Originally, however, the roof's perfectly abstract pyramid shape must have been at least in part corrected by projecting ribs running down the edges. These were removed during the 1898-1907 restoration scheme. At that time, the staircase leading up to the lantern was also moved from its original location on the roof's east side, facing the Cathedral.

The Portals

The main entrances to the Baptistery are on the south, north and east sides. Between the 14th and 15th centuries each was fitted with a set of spectacular gilt bronze doors. The portals themselves had existed from the earliest times, because they met the specific requirements relating to the rite of baptism. They were probably originally equipped with wooden doors. The south and north portals were flanked by pairs of columns made of blocks of green serpentine placed one above the other. The main entrance was framed by white marble monoliths – probably recovered from a Roman site – and flanked by two ancient

At either side of the apse's exterior wall, the corner spouts portray stylized lions devouring anthropomorphic masks (above: the spout at the south-west corner). These figures were fashioned in the 13th century, and recall the passage in the Psalms which beseeches God to save man from the snare of the Evil One, symbolized by the lion's jaws ("Salva me de ore leonis", or "save me from the lion's mouth", Ps. 22,21).

columns of red porphyry. The latter are both incomplete and in poor condition. Porphyry was a rare stone, which the Romans imported from Egypt and used for building. In the Middle Ages it came to symbolize the sacred character of ancient Rome. The Republic of Pisa presented these two columns to Florence in the 12th century, as a token of gratitude for this city's help in fighting the Saracens. Knocked down by one of Florence's many floods, they were hooped and placed against the Baptistery's east side.

The Baptistery's exterior panelling was completed in the 13th century. The work to embellish the exterior with statuary began in the 1300s and lasted for the better part of two centuries.

The Sculptures above the Portals

Baptism of Christ (East Portal)

The 'epic' phase in the decoration of the Baptistery's exterior and interior came to an end in the 15th century, when Lorenzo Ghiberti completed his two sets of bronze doors. But the contribution of later ages is far from irrelevant. During the 16th century, the three portals were given a worthy complement with the new statues installed above them and depicting scenes linked to the building's function and to its patron Saint.

For two centuries the east portal had been surmounted by Tino di Camaino's *St John the Baptist and the Theological Virtues*. But Renaissance taste – in the words of a contemporary document – proclaimed these Gothic statues "clumsy", as well as "weather-worn". In 1502 the officials of Arte di Calimala accepted a proposal put forward by Andrea Sansovino (ca. 1467-1529) to replace the old statues with a new group portraying the *Baptism of Christ*. The baptism scene, a key element in the iconographic cycle of St John the Baptist's Life, was already depicted in Tino di Camaino's group of statues filling the tri-

On the Baptistery's east façade is a niche which once contained the marble group depicting the Baptism of Christ. *Probably designed in 1505 by Andrea Sansovino himself, it consists of two Corinthian columns supporting an architrave. The door is flanked by columns of red porphyry. According to tradition, the columns were a gift offered by Pisa in 1117 for the Florentines' help in fighting the Saracens in the Balearic Islands. Up to 1424, as we can see on the panel on the wedding chest at the Bargello Museum (→ p. 13), they were placed at a distance of 5 metres from the façade, to frame the door. Felled by a violent rainstorm in 1429, they were hooped and placed in their current location.*

partite niche above the south portal. A painted chest of 1430, done by Giovanni Toscani, attests this fact (see p. 13). The surviving pieces of this work (see p. 114) are now at Opera del Duomo. Three years after starting the job, the much sought-after Sansovino departed for Rome, leaving his work unfinished. They remained in this state for more than fifty years, until the Perugia artist Vincenzo Danti (1530-1576) was entrusted to complete them. Installed in 1569, they were 'temporarily' accompanied by a stucco angel, which Innocenzo Spinazzi (1726-1798) replaced with a marble angel in 1792, an event recorded in an inscription at the foot of the statue.

Although the presence of an angel at the baptism scene is linked to an ancient and well-established iconographic tradition, this was not part of Sansovino's original project. His was a bold and innovative conception, designed to dramatically concentrate the action on the two images of St John and Christ. We are not sure how much of the group was actually completed by Sansovino himself, and how much can be attributed to Danti. Sansovino is usually credited with the conception of the figures. Like in his other works, here too the artist brings together a gently turning figure (Christ) and a second figure (St John), whose body faces the viewer but whose head is seen from the side. Scholars generally agree that Sansovino himself may have carved the latter image. The dynamic flow of the robes and the Saint's striking head seem purposely to echo the style of the Ghiberti doors below. Most of the figure of Christ can, on the other hand, be attributed to Danti; though accurately shaped, it does not display the forceful modelling and play of light we see in its companion.

During World War II this group, as well as other important statues, were removed from their location and kept in a sheltered place till the end of hostilities. Photographs taken in those years show that the statues were undamaged and in generally good condition. In the summer of 1975 the Christ's right arm, which had been corroded in two spots by acid rains, fell off the statue and hit the ground where it was dashed to pieces. A decision was taken to restore the group of statues and to protect them from air pollution. The originals, now at Opera del Duomo Museum, have been replaced on the exterior of the Baptistery with lime and marble dust copies.

In 1502 Andrea Sansovino received a commission from Arte di Calimala to sculpt a Baptism of Christ, to replace Tino di Camaino's 13th century marble group of the Virtues and St John the Baptist on the east façade of the Baptistery. But the sculptor left Florence three years later, leaving his work unfinished except for the figure of St John (above). In 1569 Vincenzo Danti concluded the figure of Christ, but the group was completed only in 1792, when Innocenzo Spinazzi added the figure of the angel.

St John the Baptist's Sermon (North Portal)

Shortly after commissioning Sansovino to do the two statues of the *Baptism of Christ*, the Calimala Guild officials resolved to finance a new set of sculptures for the north door as well. The object was to replace Tino di Camaino's statuary with "handsome bronze figures… to match the bronze doors of the church". The theme of Tino's composition, *St John the Baptist's Sermon*, was to remain unchanged. The Saint, in a central position, is intent on lecturing the Pharisee and the Levite who stand on either side of him.

It was Giovan Francesco Rustici (1475-1554) who in 1506 secured the commission for this group of three statues. In keeping with the contract, the artist undertook to finish the statues in two years, but by 1509 he had only completed the preliminary terracotta models. Rustici entrusted the bronze casting of the group to Bernardino da Mi-

The north portal, surmounted by Giovan Francesco Rustici's Sermon of St John the Baptist, commissioned in 1506. The bronze group was unveiled on 24 June, 1511, standing inside a niche also designed by Rustici. The latter consists of two fluted Corinthian colonnettes supporting an architrave and resting on square plinths decorated with the Calimala eagle. In his "Lives of the Painters, Sculptors and Architects", Vasari suggests that Leonardo da Vinci may have contributed to the execution of these models. He goes on to describe the statues minutely, and praises them for being the "most perfect and best conceived ever to have been made by a modern master". The inscriptions on the pedestals record a dialogue narrated in the Gospel According to St John (1, 21-23). Queried by the priests of Jerusalem as to his identity and mission, St John the Baptist answers: "I am a voice crying in the wilderness: make straight the way of the Lord!" Thus he echoes the words of the prophet Isaiah who prophesied that one day this man would preach in the desert of Judaea. In this well-known passage, St John the Baptist announces the Coming of the Messiah, declaring himself unworthy of so much as undoing His sandals. In a similar story told by St Matthew (3, 8-12), St John the Baptist calls on the multitudes to repent, while awaiting the One who will baptize them not with simple water, but with the Holy Ghost, and with fire.

lano, a specialist in the field. The finished work was unveiled on St John's Day, 1511. The balance of the payment, amounting to 1200 florins, was paid to Rustici in 1523.

On the pedestals supporting the statues we read the dialogue in Hebrew between the three figures. "What will you tell me?" asks the bearded Pharisee standing to the left of St John. The bald Levite to his right exclaims: "Who are you? Elias?" The Baptist declares to them and to the crowd of the faithful: "A voice cries out in the wilderness: make straight the way [of the Lord]!" Vasari warmly praises the three figures, which he says are "done with tremendous elegance and skill", and mentions that the sculptor apparently enjoyed the constant assistance of Leonardo, who, like Rustici, had been trained in Andrea del Verrocchio's workshop. The story might well have some truth to it, for in 1508 Leonardo was indeed in Florence, and because in some ways Rustici's bronze figures – particularly that of the Levite ("a portly and very well done figure with a bald head", says Vasari) – do remind us closely of some of Leonardo's caricature drawings. Furthermore, like Leonardo's celebrated *Last Supper* in Milan, *St John the Baptist's Sermon* also brings together its highly expressive figures in an intense mutual relationship. The Hebrew words at the foot of the statues – probably contributed by some erudite scholar of the times, but well-nigh incomprehensible to most people – certainly do little to illustrate the meaning of this episode in the Baptist's life. Rather, the scene strives to convey its message through the stance adopted by the two bystanders – who are inquisitorial and puzzled at the same time – and through the prophetic self-assurance of the Lord's Envoy.

Rustici also cast a bronze eagle, the Arte di Calimala emblem. It stands above the central window in the second order, looking fiercely predatory. We meet this heraldic animal again on the two square-

shaped plinths which support the architraved Corinthian columns standing against the wall. These architectural elements frame Rustici's statues, and are similar to those framing Sansovino's *Baptism*, which were being completed at roughly the same time.

Beheading of St John the Baptist (South Portal)

The commission for a third and last group of statues for the south door went to the sculptor Vincenzo Danti more than fifty years later, when he was finishing Sansovino's *Baptism*. Danti's work was to replace Tino di Camaino's abovementioned marble group, which depicted the scene of the baptism. For this portal the choice fell on the *Beheading of the Baptist*, a subject that had not been treated in Tino's cycle. Like its companion groups above the Baptistery's other two portals, this one is also made up three figures. St John the Baptist is seen kneeling at the centre, submitting to the blade wielded by the executioner, with Salome witnessing the scene. The three large statues were cast in 1570 and set up the following year. The round bronze pedestals on which they stand are decorated with allegorical images in low relief of *Lust* (Salome), the *Three Theological Virtues* (St John the Baptist), and *Intemperance* (the Executioner).

Vincenzo Danti, a "truly uncommon young man, and a highly talented one", in Vasari's judgement, came to Florence in 1557, and worked primarily for Grand Duke Cosimo I as a sculptor in bronze and marble. The regard in which he was held in Florence must have prompted Calimala's senior officials to entrust him with the bronze group. They are conceived with a dynamic tension and vitality which calls to mind Giambologna, who was the most influential figure in Florentine sculpture at that time. The refined Mannerist taste, then very popular at the Medici court, can be detected especially in Salome's somewhat affected and aristocratic elegance. Her finely

Vincenzo Danti, Beheading of St John the Baptist *(1569-1570). The 16th-century chronicler Giovanni Lapini states that this sculptural group was unveiled above the Baptistery's south portal on June 22nd 1571, two days before St John's Day. Allegories decorate the pedestals of the three statues: Lust at Salome's feet, Intemperance at the executioner's feet, while St John the Baptist is symbolized by the Three Theological Virtues. The work is a typical product of Mannerism, and chronologically the last of the groups sculpted for the Baptistery's exterior.*

Andrea Pisano's bronze doors went to fill the east portal of the Baptistery (facing the main entrance to the Cathedral) in 1336. In 1424 they were shifted to the south portal, to make way for the first set of bronze doors fashioned by Lorenzo Ghiberti. The first document mentioning the name of the author of the doors is dated 22 January, 1329 (actually 1330, for the Florentine calendar began the new year on 25 March, the day of the Annunciation). On 2 April of the same year the wax models were ready, but the actual casting was completed only in April 1332. Andrea Pisano and his assistants then set to work to gild and finish chasing the bronze relief panels. The doors are covered with 28 quatrefoil frames containing scenes from the life and martyrdom of St John the Baptist, and allegories of the Cardinal and Theological Virtues.

carved robes and hair are clearly an effort to express on a larger scale the fine work of the goldsmith, for this was the art in which Danti had initially been trained.

The Bronze Doors

Andrea Pisano's Doors (South Portal)

The oldest of the Baptistery's three pairs of bronze doors has the date 1330 recorded on it. Andrea da Pontedera, better known as Andrea Pisano (1290/95-1349), started work on the doors in this year, and completed them in 1336. At that time they were installed in the building's east portal, facing the Cathedral, but were moved to the south portal in 1424, to make way for Lorenzo Ghiberti's first set of doors.

In Pisano's oeuvre, each door leaf is divided into 14 squares, totalling 28 scenes. This includes 20 episodes taken from the life of St John the Baptist, and eight allegorical figures depicting the Virtues. The succession of episodes on each door goes from left to right and from top to bottom. On the left-hand door are: 1) *The Birth of St John the Baptist is Announced to Zechariah*; 2) *Zechariah is Struck Dumb*; 3) *Visitation*; 4) *Birth of St John*; 5) *Naming of St John*; 6) *The Youthful St John in the Wilderness*; 7) *St John Preaches to the Multitudes*; 8) *St John Announces the Coming of Christ*; 9) *St John Blesses the Crowds*; 10) *Baptism of Christ*. On the right-hand door we see: 11) *St John Before King Herod*; 12) *St John is Thrown into Prison*; 13) *The Disciples Visit St John in Prison*; 14) *St John's Disciples Witness Christ's Miracles*; 15) the *Dance of Salome*; 16) *Beheading of St John*; 17) *St John's Head is Shown to King Herod*; 18) *Salome Shows the Head to Herodias*; 19) *St John's Body Carried to the Grave*; 20) *Burial Scene*.

On the two bottom levels are the allegorical representations of the Four Cardinal Virtues and the Three Theological Virtues: the addition of *Humility* was probably made to lend greater harmony to the composition. Nevertheless, this allegorical figure is very much to the point in a cycle devoted to St John the Baptist, for in the New Testament he declared his insignificance before Christ the Saviour. The Virtues, represented by a winged figure (Hope) and seven seated female figures bearing emblems, include: *Hope, Faith, Fortitude* and *Temperance* on the left door, and *Charity, Humility, Justice* and *Prudence* on the right door. Both the stories and the allegories are wrought in gilt bronze and encased within mixtilinear quatrefoil frames, following a model that was much used in Gothic met-

*Andrea Pisano's doors filling
the Baptistery's south portal
(also called "the Gates of Mercy",
after the old charitable institution
located on the square facing it)
narrate the story of St John the
Baptist with a wealth of details
only exceeded by the late 15th
century Vestments of St John the
Baptist (→ p. 121). The scenes
depicted by this great artist are
arranged according to a precise
order. On the left we see the
episodes pertaining to St John's
sermons and his public life, while
on the right are those dealing
with his martyrdom and the events
taking place after his death.
On this page, starting from the top
left-hand corner:* The Birth of
St John the Baptist is Announced
to Zechariah, St John the Baptist
Blesses the Multitudes *and* The
Baptism of Christ *(left wing);*
The Beheading of St John the
Baptist, St John's Body Carried
to the Grave *(right wing).
In the lower part of the doors
are the Three Theological Virtues:*
Hope, Faith *(left wing),* and
Charity *(right wing). Andrea
Pisano's own contemporaries,
we are told in the Chronicle kept
by the Calimala official Giovanni
Villani, found "the metal doors
of Santo Giovanni exceedingly
lovely, and awe-inspiring in terms
of work and cost". In fashioning
them, Andrea Pisano drew
inspiration not only from the
mosaics in the Baptistery, but
also from Giotto's frescoes in the
Peruzzi Chapel at Santa Croce.
Vasari makes the same point,
adding that Andrea brought
about a stylistic reform, having
duly "considered Giotto's new
technique and the few ancient
things that were known to him".
Following the example of this
great painter and architect,
Andrea achieved a clear and
succinct style. The sober restraint
expressed in the Beheading is one
of its most poignant examples.*

The Three Theological Virtues are followed by Humility *(on the left) – not, strictly speaking, one of the canonical series of Virtues. And yet this is no casual addition, for St John the Baptist always cultivated humility, both in his life and in his sermons. Indeed, we have only to think of the passage in the New Testament (see above), in which he declares his insignificance before of the Messiah – He who will come to baptize the people with the fire of the Holy Ghost, and "separate the wheat from the chaff", sending the elect to Paradise and sinners to hellfire and eternal damnation. The cycle ends with four Cardinal Virtues:* Fortitude, Temperance, Justice *and* Prudence *(right).*

al-work. This scheme may be ascribed to Andrea's early training as a goldsmith. (Ghiberti used the same background 70 years later for his first set of bronze doors for the Baptistery.) On the decorative bands that divide the two door leafs into 28 squares, are 48 reliefs of lions' heads. This was a traditional motif appearing on medieval bronze doors, for the lion symbolically protected holy places.

Even though artists in those times did not usually sign their creations, these doors were such a distinguished and innovative work that Andrea Pisano carved the following words in gilt letters at the top: ANDREAS : UGOLINI : NINI : DE : PISIS : ME : FECIT : A : D : M : CCC : XXX: "Andrea (son) of Ugolino (son of) Nino of Pisa fashioned me in the year 1330". The Pisan master was justly proud of his accomplishment, not only because of the sheer beauty and grandeur of these doors, which had been given a finish to make them look like a monumental piece of gold-work, but also because of the innovative technology involved in casting them. It had been nearly two centuries since the last great bronze doors – gilt bronze to boot – had been fashioned in Italy. Not for nothing had the Arte di Calimala chiefs initially considered replacing the old wooden doors with a fresh set of wooden doors encased within metal sheets. But in 1329 the officials went ahead with a more ambitious project of casting the doors entirely in bronze, and gilding parts of them, to make them "as beautiful as possible". This was not the first time that Florentine artists rose to meet a new technical challenge. A century earlier they had successfully decorated the Baptistery dome with mosaics, using the technique of tessera-setting which had no precedent in the city's artistic tradition.

Art lovers for sure, but also shrewd and practical-minded as all merchants should be, the Florentines prepared this undertaking with a good deal of care. They first sent a connoisseur, the goldsmith Piero di Jacopo, to Pisa to draw the bronze doors of the Cathedral. Made by Bonanno Pisano in the 12th century, these were the only such doors existing in Tuscany at that time. Although the artistic level of sculpture in Tuscany had certainly not fallen in the intervening period, the difficult techniques of casting bronze had indeed been forgotten. But they were known in Venice, thanks to this city's closer ties with the Byzantine Empire, the latter having inherited much of the ancient world's proficiency in the technical sciences.

Piero di Jacopo then went to Venice to meet local specialists and to engage the services of the master Leonardo d'Avanzo, who came to Florence in 1332 to join Andrea Pisano in making the doors. Andrea had in fact already been chosen as "Master of the Doors" due to his training as a goldsmith and consequent expertise in the processing of metals, but also because he was considered a major sculptor of his times, with a style strikingly akin to Giotto's.

Although a native of Pisa, where sculpture had been strongly marked by the dramatic force of Giovanni Pisano's works, Andrea's own artistic language was closer to Giotto's, and to the more classicizing French Gothic style which had influenced Giotto himself. So deeply does Andrea appear to be imbued with the French manner, that we can safely guess that he spent some time in France. This is not at all far-fetched, for at that time there was much more contact between the Italian peninsula and the countries of northern Europe than is supposed today.

Giotto's influence shaped Andrea's classical Gothic style, making it simpler and more effective. Set against architectural and natural backgrounds, which are sober but owe much to that master's spatial conception, the episodes appear quite natural and credible to us. The figures and narrative elements exemplifying the events that take place in each scene are presented with almost didactic clarity, and are devoid of descriptive or ornamental digressions. Here the artist – who had been trained to master the 'ornate' manner of the goldsmith, based on decorative minutiae – adapts wonderfully to the clarity required in a work to be taken in at a glance from a distance. Upon examining the fine quality of the reliefs more carefully, however, we immediately

Above: although the formal elegance of Andrea Pisano's allegorical rendition of the Virtues has no precedent, scholars have nonetheless drawn attention to their similarity to Giotto's conception, in particular the latter's figure of Hope in Padua's Scrovegni Chapel.
Left: Andrea Pisano, who had been trained as a goldsmith, borrowed the decorative quatrefoil design of French origin, but used it innovatively and on a vaster scale.
On the contrary, the forty-eight lion heads appearing at the sides of the relief frames to symbolically guard the Baptistery are a traditional decorative element.

The contract for a set of doors to fill the north portal (also called "Gates of the Cross") was signed by Ghiberti and his father on 23 November, 1403. Under its terms, the artist was to be paid 200 florins per year to fashion three relief panels within the same period of time – a very good sum indeed, when compared to the normal levels of remuneration in those days. But in 1407 Calimala officials drew up a stricter contract, probably because Ghiberti was not punctual in handing in his work. In 1424 the doors – which had cost 22,000 florins, a sum equal to the annual defence budget for the city of Florence – were set up in the east portal of the Baptistery. They were replaced here in 1452 by Ghiberti's second set of doors, or "Gates of Paradise". The artist's first oeuvre follows the model established by Andrea Pisano. His twenty-eight relief panels, set within quatrefoil frames, narrate the life of Christ and depict the Evangelists and the Fathers of the Church. To shape the panels, he used a soft alloy casting technique.

identify them as the work of a goldsmith. Andrea models the shapes with rhythmic elegance and subtly carves the minor decorative details. Examples are the drapery on the altar in *The Birth of St John the Baptist is Announced to Zechariah*, or the ornate chairs on which the delicately feminine figures of the Virtues are seated.

The layers of grime which today coat and dim Andrea Pisano's work make it difficult to analyze the details. A much needed restoration program will allow us to study them more closely, although it may not be able to bring out the splendour of the original gilding, which in many spots has been damaged by the hands of visitors. Indeed, the shiny areas here and there on the doors are not gold, but only the brass contained in the bronze alloy.

If Andrea Pisano's doors today still appear to us as a piece of extraordinary workmanship, we can imagine how much more beautiful they must have seemed to the Florentines who saw them being fitted into the Baptistery's east portal. The enthusiastic comments in contemporary chronicles testify to this excitement. One 14th century commentator, Simone della Tosa, reports: "all Florence rushed to see the bronze Doors wrought by Andrea Pisano for San Giovanni… And all the city elders, seldom seen outside the Palace for all but the most formal events, came with the Ambassadors of the two crowns of Naples and Sicily to see them being raised up, and rewarded Andrea for all his labours with citizenship of Florence". In his *Cronica*, Giovanni Villani proudly reminds us that he was charged by Arte di Calimala to follow the progress on "the metal doors… exceedingly beautiful, and impressive in terms of both labour and cost".

In composing the 20 *Stories of St John the Baptist*, the artist followed the iconographic models which were already established in Florence at that time, such as the mosaics on the Baptistery dome and Giotto's frescoes in Santa Croce's Peruzzi Chapel. But this was the first time that the life of Florence's patron Saint had been narrated with such a wealth of details. This perfectly balanced diptych fully covers his life and his sermons (left door), as well as his martyrdom and death (right door).

Ghiberti's First Set of Doors (North Portal)

The awe occasioned by the stylistic and technical success of Andrea Pisano's doors had an enduring effect. In 1401 the authorities announced a competition for a second pair of bronze doors for the Baptistery. The terms stated that the winner would be expected to follow the structure and general features of Andrea's work. The two door wings and the framework for the individual panels were to be cast in one solid piece of bronze with a silky finish, while the scenes in relief were to be done one at a time and gilded with mercury amalgam before being fitted into the doors.

From left to right and from the top working downwards: between the Evangelists and the Fathers of the Church, which Ghiberti depicted on the north doors, are St Matthew, St John, St Augustine (left wing), and St Gregory the Great (right wing). These relief panels are thought to have been carved between 1407 and 1413. Below: a detail of the reverse side of the doors. Here Lorenzo Ghiberti added the decorative motif of the lion busts, already used by Andrea Pisano.

The doors we see today on the Baptistery's north side were originally designed to replace Andrea Pisano's doors on the east portal, opposite the Cathedral. They are the work of Lorenzo Ghiberti (1378-1455), who did them between 1403 and 1424. Following Pisano's scheme, they are also divided into 28 small reliefs. 20 of them narrate *Stories from the New Testament*, while the remaining eight portray the Fathers of the Church and the Evangelists. Each multifoil panel is set within a garlanded frame with heads of prophets in each corner (48 in all) done in high relief. Contrary to the traditional scheme, Ghiberti arranged his scenes working from the bottom up and from left to right, with the story sequence extending horizontally across both wings.

Two decorative bands run across the bottom of both doors. In the lower one are the four Fathers of the Church, *St Augustine, St Jerome, St Gregory the Great* and *St Ambrose*, seated at writing tables, while the upper band portrays the four Evangelists, *John, Matthew, Luke* and *Mark*. The compartments from the third level up contain New Testament scenes in high relief, including: 1) the *Annunciation*; 2) the *Nativity*; 3) *Adoration of the Magi*; 4) *Christ Among the Doctors*; 5) *Baptism of Christ*; 6) *Temptation in the Wilderness*; 7) *Christ Driving the Money-Changers from the Temple*; 8) *Christ Walking on the Water*; 9) *Transfiguration*; 10) *Resurrection of Lazarus*; 11) *Entry into Jerusalem*; 12) the *Last Supper*; 13) *Prayer in the Garden of Gethsemane*; 14) *Christ is Captured*; 15) the *Flagellation*; 16) *Christ before Pilate*; 17) the *Road to Calvary*; 18) *Crucifixion*; 19) the *Resurrection*; 20) *Pentecost*.

Above: from left to right: the compartments portraying the Annunciation (left wing), Jesus Amongst the Doctors (right wing) and the Baptism of Christ (left wing). Ghiberti put his signature above the Nativity and the Adoration of the Magi ("Opus Laurentii Florentinii" – the work of Lawrence the Florentine). Scholars estimate that the panels were completed before the year 1407. Assistants to the work included the likes of Masolino, Donatello, Michelozzo and Paolo Uccello. In this sense, Ghiberti's workshop became a crucible where the transition between the International Gothic style and the early Renaissance took place. Nevertheless, the style of the doors, already full of citations of classical models (thus foreshadowing the new spirit of Humanism), is emphatically Ghiberti's very own.

Since the Calimala Guild had initially considered having the new doors decorated with stories from the Old Testament, the participants in the competition were asked to submit trial reliefs depicting the Sacrifice of Isaac. But, as is clear from the 1403 contract signed by the winner, Lorenzo Ghiberti, the merchants finally opted for a cycle of stories from the life of Christ. In this way they sought to establish a link with Andrea Pisano's narration of the life of St John the Baptist. The death of him who had "paved the way for the Coming of Christ", marks the beginning of the era of Christ the Saviour of humanity, of Him who was "the Gate to Salvation", in John the Evangelist's words. Thus the doors facing the Cathedral are the *ianua salutis* – "gate to salvation" – for two reasons: 1) they illustrate the central position occupied by Christ in the history of the redemption of humankind, and 2) it is through them that the faithful may enter into the Baptistery, there to be cleansed of the original sin and start on the path to salvation.

Ghiberti's reliefs draw on the vast iconographic repertory covering the life and works of Christ, concentrating on the most basic events, those that most eloquently establish the human and divine nature of Christ, His death and resurrection, and His continuity in the Church. Of the many miracles narrated in the Gospels, only two are illustrated, so as to underscore the fact that only through the true faith (*Christ Walking on the Water*) can a human being be resurrected from the living death of sin to the life eternal (*Resurrection of Lazarus*). All knowledge of Christ is based on the testimony of the Gospels (the *Evangelists* in the bottom row), and on its critical interpretation by the founders of Christian theology (the *Fathers of the Church* in the next row up). The 48 high relief heads of the *Prophets*, *Prophetesses* and *Sibyls* in the corners add pregnancy to the prediction of the Messiah's coming, and reaffirm the role of Man in the history of Salvation. The artist substituted these heads for the traditional lion busts of ancient art (which he did, however, portray on the back of the doors, at the centre of the studs corresponding to each panel). On the left door leaf, above the third level from the bottom, the central head stands out both for its realism and for the strikingly modern style of its headgear and garments. A reliable tradition has it that this is a portrait of Lorenzo Ghiberti himself.

Following Andrea Pisano's example, Ghiberti also added his signature to his oeuvre. The inscription above the panels of the *Annunciation* and the *Adoration of the Magi* reads: OPUS LAURENTII FLORENTINI ("the work of Lawrence the Florentine"). And of course the artist had every reason to be proud of his work, which "he had conducted with exceeding skill and discipline", as he himself briefly says in his *Commentari*. He devotes more space to the competition in which he prevailed over a number of other well-known artists, and which even so many years later appeared to him a recognition of his abilities and the starting point of his rise to artistic prominence. It is not by chance that Ghiberti himself – and Vasari later, as well – should put the accent on the novelty and perfection of this accomplishment, which is first and foremost an example of technical prowess. This is all the more true if we consider that a century earlier Andrea Pisano's doors had required the support of Venetian metallurgical experts. In ways that are not clear to us, Ghiberti successfully mastered the casting of large-scale bronze works, a technique that was still new to the Florence of his time. Ghiberti gave another demonstration of his surpassing skill in this field when he fashioned the great statue of *St John the Baptist* for a niche on the exterior of Orsanmichele church – the first, but already perfect, example of bronze statuary produced in Florence.

Ghiberti's training as a goldsmith also gave him the skills required for the delicate work that followed the casting. The reliefs came out of the furnace rough cast, and all details had to be painstakingly finished with burin and chisel. It was probably knowledge of this craft that gave Ghiberti mastery over all the latest techniques of the International Gothic, for it was in the production of gold objects that these techniques gave the best results and helped spread new artistic ideas. While in the reliefs on the Baptistery doors this influence appears to be muted by experiences in other fields, it comes out very clearly in

In the scenes from the Life of Christ, the images depicting the divine epiphanies and miracles worked by the Messiah are alternated with the story narrating how the Saviour took the shape of man and suffered the Passion. Below, from left to right and from the top working down, are Temptation in the Wilderness, Christ Walking on the Water, Entry into Jerusalem, The Capture of Christ, The Road to Calvary *and* The Resurrection.

Opposite page: the heads of prophets and prophetesses at the corners of the panels on Ghiberti's first set of doors, replace Andrea Pisano's lion head motifs. It was these Old Testament figures who prophesied the bestowing of Divine Grace upon man, which is the theme depicted in the relief panels. Below: the prophet at the centre of the left wing is said to be Ghiberti's self-portrait.

the admirable naturalistic details on the panel frames. The vibrant and elegantly acuminate foliage harbours a realistic bestiary of insects and small animals that intrigue the viewer and lead him from surprise to surprise.

Contemporary sources allow us to reconstruct fairly precisely the laborious stages of this undertaking, which took over twenty years to complete. In November 1403 Arte di Calimala entrusted the task to "the goldsmiths Lorenzo di Bartolo and his father Bartolo di Michele". Under the terms of the contract, Ghiberti was allowed to seek his father's help, and that of "other suitable masters", but he would be personally responsible for executing "figures, trees and similar things on the reliefs", producing three panels per year. In spite of considerable outside help (an official document drawn up after 1404 lists 11 such cases, including Donatello's assistance), the job progressed more slowly than foreseen. This is clear from a second contract in 1407 which imposed stricter conditions on Ghiberti, requesting him to be present every day in the workshop or waive the agreed yearly payment of 200 florins. Thereafter the instances of outside help rose to 21, and work proceeded so briskly that in 1412-1413 Ghiberti received permission from the merchants' guild to take on other commitments. By the end of 1415 almost all the panels – or *compassi* as they are called in the official documents of the time (a reference to the frames encasing them) – had been completed, but it took additional years to polish the bronze, cast the door leafs, gild the reliefs and fit them into their frames. The doors were set up in the portal opposite Santa Maria del Fiore on Easter day, 1424. The undertaking had cost more than 16,000 florins, a colossal figure for those days. Only in Florence was it possible to invest such a high sum for a single work of art.

During those two decades, Ghiberti's workshop not only produced a masterpiece; it also fuelled the further development of Florentine art. Artists like Donatello, Michelozzo, Paolo Uccello and Masolino contributed to this project, and by sharing ideas with the master they derived new insights for their own work. In spite of the outside help given by artists with such forceful personalities, in every detail of the doors we detect the unmistakable imprint of Ghiberti's own style. As the foremost representative of the International Gothic in Florence in his day, Ghiberti had felicitously blended a studied elegance in form with a charmingly natural story-telling manner. The square shape of the quatrefoil frame (which in the trial relief was developed vertically, following Andrea Pisano's example) allowed Ghiberti to organize the space within the frame in a more balanced way. The story is always presented on a supporting plane, which for the outdoor scenes is a rocky platform, and for the interiors a short projecting plane supported by brackets of classical design. The architectural design is also classicizing – indeed we detect in it a gradual progression towards a more faithful representation of ancient architecture. A typical instance of this is the contrast between the simple niche sheltering a bashful Virgin Mary in the *Annunciation*, and the solemn Corinthian portico in the *Flagellation*.

Although featuring an overall unity of style, we detect variations in these reliefs that seem to reflect the evolving artistic climate in Tus-

cany at that time. This fact has led scholars to divide the Ghiberti stories into a number of clearly defined chronological periods. The first
group, including the *Annunciation*, the *Nativity*, *Adoration of the Magi*, *Baptism of Christ* and *Prayer in the Garden of Gethsemane*, is characterized by a much stronger Gothic accent in the rhythmical flow of
the drapery and the sheer perspective, which occupies most of the
space inside the frame. The panels of the second group (*Christ among
the Doctors*, *Temptation in the Wilderness*, *Transfiguration*, the *Last
Supper* and *Crucifixion*) were probably completed sometime between
1407 and 1413. They are remarkable for a soft rhythmical quality of
the figures, which seems to temper the pathos in the scene. Here the
composition has been more deftly adapted to the constrictions of the
quatrefoil outlines. The reliefs at the foot of the doors (the *Evangelists*
and the *Fathers of the Church*) probably belong to this same period, when Ghiberti's workshop received a lot of outside
help. The third group of reliefs, executed after 1414,
demonstrates a growing freedom from the rigid narrative structure. This group includes *Christ Driving the Money-Changers from the Temple*, *Entry
into Jerusalem*, *Christ before Pilate*, *Resurrection
of Lazarus*, *Christ Walking on the Water* and the
Resurrection. Thanks also to the wealth of figures
and the attention paid to minor details, these scenes
represent situations just as they are unfolding, and
are thus highly dynamic. The distinctive features of the
last group (*Christ is Captured*, the *Flagellation*, the *Road
to Calvary* and *Pentecost*) allow us to detect an artistic
maturity in Ghiberti that reached its high point in
the 'Gates of Paradise'. Here the composition
hinges on a central element round which the
entire composition is seen to revolve. The spatial effects widen the scenes and deepen the perspective, while the architectural details and the human
figures bear a classicizing imprint.

Opposite page: the original pair of doors filling the Baptistery's east portal, before they were shifted to Opificio in 1990 for restoration. According to Vasari, Michelangelo praised Ghiberti's work in words which were to become proverbial: "They are so lovely they could grace the entrance to Paradise". Scholars, however, point out that the main doors of all holy places were, from ancient times, given the same name – Gates of Paradise. The contract assigning the job to Ghiberti was signed by him on 2 January, 1425, but the doors were not completed till 1452. In a letter of 24 June, 1424, addressed to the Calimala official Niccolò da Uzzano, the Chancellor of the Florentine Republic Leonardo Bruni detailed an iconographic program which followed the scheme of the earlier pairs of doors, with twenty-eight compartments depicting episodes from the Old Testament and the Books of the Prophets. This initial arrangement is revealed on the reverse side of the doors, where we indeed see a subdivision into twenty-eight sections. However, thanks to the success of his earlier doors, Ghiberti was capable of pushing through his own choice, consisting of large rectangular panels in the new Renaissance taste. He had already experimented with this format when designing the new baptismal font for the city of Siena. Some scholars believe that he turned to the Humanist Ambrogio Traversari for help, and was further inspired by Bishop Antonino. Be that as it may, he worked out a new narrative scheme for the doors, compressing the Biblical stories – from Genesis through the Book of Kings – into a total of ten panels. Thus each panel develops a number of different episodes. This innovation actually goes back to Siena's 13th century landscape painters, and was used in a masterly way by Masaccio in his Brancacci Chapel frescoes (church of Santa Maria del Carmine, Florence). Ghiberti also used relief studies prepared by Brunelleschi and Donatello. From the latter he borrowed the stiacciato ("flattened out") relief technique, in which the projection of the more distant objects is progressively reduced.

Often overshadowed by its 'elder sister', the 'Gates of Paradise', Ghiberti's first doors remain an unparalleled masterpiece, both in artistic and technical terms. Thanks to them, Florentine – and even European – art forged well ahead of the last and noblest expressions of the great Gothic tradition, in the direction of Humanism.

Ghiberti's 'Gates of Paradise' (East Portal)

In 1425, one year after Ghiberti had laboriously completed the doors described above, the consuls of Arte di Calimala commissioned "the excellent master" to fashion a second set of doors. These were designed to fill the main portal facing the Cathedral, and have always been known as the 'Gates of Paradise'. According to Vasari, this definition was coined by Michelangelo himself, and aptly sums up their exquisite beauty. But since in those times the main portal leading to a place of worship was often referred to as the 'Gates of Paradise', we cannot be sure that the term is not of specifically religious origin.

There is no doubt, however, that from the very first day they were set up, the doors were greeted with universal acclaim. This is further confirmed by the fact that in July 1452 Ghiberti's earlier doors were moved to the north portal, to give this freshly completed set the place of honour. Indeed, they remained facing the Cathedral for almost five and a half centuries, ever the object of unchallenged admiration. Lamentably, inappropriate refurbishing schemes and air pollution have kicked off a corrosion process underneath the gilding. In 1990 this deterioration was deemed so serious that the precious doors were removed and replaced with a gilt bronze copy.

Although the Gates of Paradise are later than the north doors, the 10 subjects they depict are Biblical – i.e., pre-Evangelical – and illustrate the themes of Salvation and the prophetic premonition in the Old Testament of the coming of Christ. Each field includes several stories. The sequence unfolds from the top downwards, and from left to right, as follows: 1) *Stories of Adam and Eve*; 2) *Stories of Cain and Abel*; 3) *Stories of Noah*; 4) *Stories of Abraham*; 5) *Stories of Jacob and Esau*; 6) *Stories of Joseph the Hebrew*; 7) *Stories of Moses*; 8) *Stories of Joshua*; 9) *Stories of David*; 10) *Stories of Solomon*.

The narrative density of the reliefs is matched by the complexity of the decorative bronze band that frames the doors. Here the fabulous Gothic naturalism found on the similar band framing the north doors gives way to the solemn depiction of Biblical figures and Prophets, in all 24 full-length figures and 24 heads that project from the niches and medallions. In one medallion on the left wing – at the centre, above the two bottom rows – Ghiberti put his self-portrait, matched on the right door by a portrait of his son Vittore, who assisted him in making the doors.

In 1424 the Humanist Leonardo Bruni formulated the initial iconographic scheme for the doors. In it he sought to establish a parallel with Ghiberti's earlier doors, by devising a sequence of 28 panels narrating stories from the Old Testament, and eight panels depicting the Prophets. This project was later altered, probably when work on the doors had already started. Indeed, the reverse sides of the doors are di-

vided into 28 squares each having a stud at the centre, and do not match the front sides. The new compositional scheme was probably Ghiberti's own; to him we can in any case ascribe a number of formal and stylistic innovations. He replaced the Gothic multifoil frame with a regular framework, in harmony with the Renaissance taste and sense of proportion. Furthermore, the narrative compactness of the ten panels is made possible by the different perspective modulations of the reliefs. Ghiberti wrote in his *Commentari*: "I was given freedom to conduct (the work) in the manner I thought most fit, to make it perfect, ornate and rich". This second undertaking was assigned to the artist without a competition – as if his creation of the first doors entitled him to do these – and it allowed Ghiberti a considerable margin of creative freedom. This shows us not only in what high esteem he was held at the time, but also the increasing consideration accorded to the artist in the new Age of Humanism. It seems probable, however, that after deciding on the compositional structure of the doors, Ghiberti was assisted by a theologian to pinpoint the narrative content of the panels, for these coherently develop the themes of sin and salvation, which had already been foreshadowed in the murder of Abel (a symbol of Christ) and the Ark of Noah (a symbol of redemption).

The first stories are followed by other stories which more explicitly illustrate the role of God as a Redeemer in the history of the Hebrew people, and foretell the coming of the Messiah. Abraham, the father of all believers, is ready to sacrifice the innocent Isaac, who symbolizes Christ. Esau passes on his birthright to Jacob, in the same way as the Gentiles will one day replace the Hebrews as the Chosen People. Joseph, who is betrayed and sold by his brothers but later forgives them, is the image of Christ's sacrifice and His mercy. Finally, the stories of Moses, Joshua and David reaffirm that salvation depends on divine intervention. The last panel, depicting the meeting of Solomon and the Queen of Sheba, can be interpreted in a more general way as the mystical wedding between Christ and the Church, as well as a direct reference to the reconciliation between the Eastern and Western Churches, ripped apart by the Schism of 1054. Indeed, after the Council of Florence of 1439, this prospect no longer appeared to be so remote.

The preparation and execution of such an ambitious oeuvre required even more time than Lorenzo Ghiberti's earlier accomplishment. A contract was signed in 1425, but it took till 1452 – 27 years later! – to finish them. During those years – a crucial time for the development of Florentine art – Ghiberti's workshop became a creative centre, churning out new ideas and technical solutions. Celebrated artists made their contributions, including Michelozzo, who collaborated between 1436 and 1442, Benozzo Gozzoli – who signed a contract in 1442 – and the likes of Luca della Robbia and Donatello, who took part in at least one of the work phases, according to an official document of

Opposite page: from left to right, and from the top working down: Stories of Adam and Eve, Stories of Cain and Abel (Opera del Duomo Museum, Florence), Stories of Noah, Stories of Abraham (Opificio delle Pietre Dure, Florence), Stories of Jacob and Esau, and Stories of Joseph the Hebrew (Opera del Duomo Museum, Florence). In the first scenes, the narration centres on the theme of sin, but in the stories of Abraham and Noah we detect the appearance of the vision of salvation through faith, which prophesies the redemption of man through such symbolic figures as Abel and Isaac. Adam and Eve are additionally portrayed in the lying figures at the top corners of the door wings. At the bottom corners are Noah and his wife. The story of Jacob (detail below) symbolizes God's censure of the Hebrews and His choosing the Gentiles as His Chosen People. The last scene is the most complex from the compositional point of view. Vasari, who considered this panel to be one of the "most artful and difficult" undertakings Ghiberti had ever attempted, points out that the temple depicted here had "with great trouble been given a perspectival twist".

From left to right, and from the top working down: Stories of Moses and Stories of Joshua (Opificio delle Pietre Dure, Florence); Stories of David and Stories of Solomon (Opera del Duomo Museum, Florence). The last three panels, as well as the Stories of Noah, are thought to date from the 1450s. The encounter between Solomon and the Queen of Sheba has been seen as an evocation of the mystical marriage of Christ and the Church, but also in the light of contemporary events, hence as an allusion to the Council of Florence and Pope Eugene IV's hopes of reuniting the Eastern and Western Churches.

1427. In the first years, progress on the doors must have been slow. In 1429 the door wings, and the frames enclosing the panels, had been cast in bronze. Ten years later, only the first five reliefs were ready. In 1443, four still remained to be made, though these were completed by 1447.

Contemporary documents, which are not always easy to interpret, lead us to believe that the panels themselves were fashioned some time between 1435 and 1445. The actual chronological sequence in which they were made has, however, not been established with any degree of certainty. It is equally difficult to ascertain to what extent certain stylistic and compositional discrepancies between one story and another are due to the intervention of outside contributors. Finally, the attempt to distinguish between the different hands is a largely fruitless pursuit, for this masterpiece must been seen as a whole, as a special blend of "solemnity… elegance and grace", as Vasari aptly expresses it, and can rightly be considered to be Ghiberti's very own contribution to the language of the Florentine Renaissance.

Those who today wish to admire the weightless contours and exquisite nudity of Eve in the *Creation*, or the spatial complexities of the *Stories of Joseph the Hebrew*, can visit the Opera del Duomo Museum and see these panels – as well as four additional ones – which have been restored to their original brilliance by the experts of Opificio delle Pietre Dure. Wrenched out of their frames by the flood waters of 1966, these six reliefs had to be re-set by making a number of holes in both door wings, and it is with them that the overall restoration program of the Gates of Paradise got underway. Its purpose is to remove the pollutants and surface encrustations, but above all to save the gilding. After so many centuries, this rests on a bed of bronze and gold oxides, which could only be eliminated by removing the surface gilt as well. It is an inevitable fact that variations in atmospheric humidity crystallize these salts, which start to bulge and eventually open up a swarm of tiny craters in the gilding. If this process were allowed to go unchecked, it would eventually make the gold disappear completely. This is why the restored portions – and, in time, the full doors – must be placed inside glass cases filled with an inert gas such as nitrogen, in an effort to stabilize the oxides upon which the gilding now rests.

In 1990, after the first four panels were removed from the doors and refurbished, the doors were shifted to the Opificio laboratories and replaced on the east portal with the copy we see today, financed by the Japanese Group Sun Motoyama. The bronze casting, done in the Fonderia Marinelli workshop, was based on a mould of the doors made after World War II. In Paris the firm Chardon et Fils gilded the reliefs by galvanization, since EU security regulations barred the mercury amalgam method employed by Ghiberti in the 15th century, on the grounds that it releases poisonous fumes.

Ornamental Frame around the North Portal

Deeply impressed by the supreme beauty of the Baptistery doors, both the hasty tourist and the more careful visitor tend to overlook the highly imaginative and delicately wrought ornamental band with which the Quattrocento framed them.

In 1423, the Ghiberti workshop produced a bronze frame for the lintel and jambs of the north portal, decorated with reliefs of creepers strewn with flowers, fruits and animals. Here Ghiberti seems to have distilled the very essence of the varied repertory of Gothic herbaria and bestiaries, fusing it all into an original creation distinguished for its lively realism and stylized elegance. At the foot of the frame we find a realistic allusion: the rings at the two corners of the lintel, which appear to support the festoons of leaves, were indeed used during celebrations to hang wreaths of flowers and fruits – a popular custom in those days. Over and above the frame's fascinating

In 1423 Ghiberti's workshop executed the decorative band in bronze that frames the north portal. The naturalistic motifs portrayed on the jambs and architrave are thought to represent the wealth of creation which is preyed upon by Evil, symbolized by the small animals hidden amongst the foliage.

decorative scheme, the animals and plants represented here are symbolically linked from ancient times to ethical and religious meanings, which are not always easy for us moderns to decipher.

Ornamental Frame around the East Portal

Ghiberti and his son Vittore fashioned the decorative band around the east portal between 1449 and 1452, employing a theme similar to the above, albeit arranged differently. The vine-creepers on the door jambs climb up out of a vase and are alternated with a twisted band. The naturalistic exuberance of the frame on the north doors, still Gothic in style, is here restrained. This is also due to the fact that in this more stylized relief the graphic subtlety seems to win over the sensuous modelling of the earlier production. At the centre of the architrave we see a Calimala eagle between two bunches of grapes, symbolizing the Eucharist. This is the only gilded portion of the relief.

Ornamental Frame around the South Portal

After the Gates of Paradise had been completed, Calimala officials commissioned Ghiberti to do a third decorative band, this time for Andrea Pisano's 14th-century doors, so that these should harmonize with the other two. The artist being now in his seventies, it was his son Vittore who completed the frame (1466). Much admired by Vasari, who called it "the rarest and most wonderful thing that one can see in bronze", this embellishment of the south portal magnifies and enhances the naturalistic wreath design of the two preceding frames, by inserting heads and figures amidst the thick vegetation. At the foot of the two jambs, the lithe beauty of the two nude figures, *Adam* and *Eve*, already seems to foreshadow the posed elegance of Mannerist bronzes.

Above: the upper section of the left door jamb, the lower section of the right jamb, and a detail of the architrave framing the Gates of Paradise (Opificio delle Pietre Dure, Florence). Lorenzo Ghiberti began work on this decorative bronze band in 1499 (1498, according to the Florentine calendar). The aged artist, aided by his son Vittore, repeated here the decorative repertory he had already used for the band framing the north portal. Right: Adam and Eve hold up the floral decoration running down the door jambs of the south portal. The execution of this band was entrusted to Lorenzo Ghiberti in 1452 and finished by his son Vittore in 1466. The latter added a number of new elements to his father's decorative scheme. Innovative ideas may also have come through a number of fresh contributors, notably Antonio del Pollaiolo.

IV. Interior

Architecture

Vasari's evaluation of the Baptistery as a whole – "measured in all its parts and perfectly carried out, endowed with all the (right) proportions" – is especially to the point when it comes to the interior. No sooner have we have stepped inside, than we can at one glance take in the harmonious unfolding of its structures. This is thanks to the building's floor plan. The great octagonal design, marked by architectural details and by the geometric inlays, suggests to us a rational conception of the interior space, lying as it does beneath the phantasmagoric, mosaic-studded dome. Like the exterior, the dominant theme inside the Baptistery is that of ancient art, in this case filtered through the early Christian models which inspired the building's precious cloak of marbles and mosaic.

The Walls of the Interior

The calculated play of shapes we see on the exterior of the Baptistery is very much echoed in the interior, which also displays a wealth of

The interior of the Baptistery: the figure of Christ the Judge occupies three registers in the west segment, thus overshadowing the whole interior of the dome. On the same side is the triumphal arch decorated with two ornamental bands. Under this arch we enter the rectangular apse, or "scarsella".

strongly plastic architectural details. On the lower storey, the lesenes on the exterior are matched inside by monumental columns in Elba granite, with gilded Corinthian capitals. They in turn support the entablature of the upper storey, following a compositional scheme derived directly from the Pantheon in Rome. Although the columns are thought by some to come from a Roman building, it is more probable that they date from the same time as the construction of the Baptistery. Elba granite was a stone rarely used by the ancients, who preferred the more prized Egyptian granite. It was, however, employed in similar ways for the Cathedral of Pisa (built a short time before the Baptistery). There is also disagreement over the origin of the fluted columns of white marble which flank the interior of the east portal, and of the four cipolin marble columns supporting the Baptistery's mosaic-sheathed *scarsella*. These persistent doubts regarding a monument which at one time Florentines believed to be wholly ancient, are in any case proof of its strongly classical character.

The Women's Gallery

On the upper storey is a wall-passage, or Women's Gallery, running along seven sides of the building and fronted by mullioned windows with two lights separated by fluted pilaster strips. Their position matches the granite columns standing below, and the pairs of fluted angle pilasters on the lower storey. On the exterior wall the gallery's presence is signalled by the green-and-white marble-patterned *loggetta*. The gallery's mullioned windows are framed at the top by inlays in groups of three, displaying geometrical designs and stylized cups, and at the bottom by pairs of mosaic panels depicting Prophets. The latter are a 14th-century addition, for originally the parapet was encased in marble slabs designed to remain in full view.

The mosaics inside the women's gallery date from the early 14th century, and cover the walls of four of its sections, or coretti. Three are located directly above the Gates of Paradise, while the fourth is

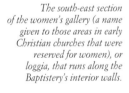

The south-east section of the women's gallery (a name given to those areas in early Christian churches that were reserved for women), or loggia, that runs along the Baptistery's interior walls.

above the south portal. In earlier times, all sections of the gallery were decorated with painted imitations of the bichrome marble inlays found elsewhere in the building.

The 'Scarsella', or Rectangular Apse

The architectural and decorative scheme of the Baptistery develops symmetrically on seven sides, but is interrupted by the *scarsella* on the wall directly opposite the main portal. The *scarsella* has a square plan, and is introduced by a majestic triumphal arch, whose two arched lintels are graced with decorative bands. Mosaic decoration spreads from the arch across to the barrel-vault over the apse. Although the year 1225 is recorded here, the mosaics in the apse were most probably done about half a century later, when decoration of the interior of the dome was in full swing (see p. 99).

The high altar stood from the earliest times in the *scarsella*. The present construction, with its parallelepiped shape and decorative inlays, is the result of a tentative reconstruction done early in the 20th century. At that time, the Baroque additions inside the building were removed, giving the Baptistery the appearance it has today. In those same years a passage was dug under the floor of the *scarsella*, on the left of the altar, to reach the excavations (at present off limits) which revealed the floor-levels of pre-existing Roman buildings.

The Drum of the Dome

Above the second storey is the drum-shaped base of the dome, resting on all eight sides of the building. Its panelling of square slabs of white marble striped with green was originally in full view, but in the early 14th century it was – like the marble parapet in the gallery – covered with mosaics, which here portray popes, bishops and deacons who were sainted.

Between the mosaic panels, splayed openings cut into the square slabs lead to the passages running inside the attic storey.

Above: one of the coretti, or sections, on the north-west side of the women's gallery. In the second half of the 13th century these areas were decorated with wall paintings imitating marble inlays. Below, the apse: at its centre is the Romanesque altar reconstructed by Giuseppe Castellucci at the beginning of the 20th century.

The celebrated mosaics covering the Baptistery dome were begun sometime in the 1200s, with work going on into the next century. On the basis of available evidence, scholars believe that the cycle can be dated to the period going from 1240 to 1310. This complex decorative iconographic program offers the faithful the story of Salvation – from Genesis down to the Last Judgement.

The Dome

Soaring above the drum, the dome constitutes the physical and ideal crowning point of the Baptistery's interior. Its majestic appearance is hardly discernible from the outside, where it is masked by the attic storey and pitched roof. The exact date of its construction is doubtful, but since the lantern is known to have been built around the middle of the 1100s, the dome is quite probably earlier. In the 13th century the eight segments that compose it were embellished with mosaics. This cycle, which took more than half a century to accomplish, depicts the *Last Judgement* and four series of episodes of sacred history. More complex and precious than painting, and yet less abstract than the intellectualized language of geometrical marble inlays, the mosaic medium was deemed well suited to illustrate the true faith with all the required power and eloquence. Thanks to it, the Baptistery's patrons also fulfilled their aim of leaving no wall of the building undecorated.

The Floor

In the early 11th century the original *cocciopesto* – crushed brick – floor was replaced with the sumptuous marble paving we see today. It covers the whole of the building's floor area, except for the region in front of the apse – the former enclosure of the presbytery – and the central octagon, which up to the 16th century was occupied by the old baptismal font. As mentioned earlier, both these medieval furnishings were demolished in 1577 and replaced with Bernardo Buontalenti's décors, to celebrate the christening of Grand Duke Francesco de' Medici's first born son (see pp. 17 and 113).

The floor comprises a series of marble 'carpets' lying side by side. Generally of rectangular or square shape, they are variously decorated with geometric patterns or figurative motifs. The materials used are white, green and red marble and stone quarried in Tuscany. The largest areas are paved with geometric patterns only, executed with the *opus tessellatum* technique, used by the craftsmen of ancient Rome. The marble pieces are medium thin, cut in regular shapes and accurately set to bring out the overall pattern.

In terms of design and execution, the inlays in the eastern area, near the Gates of Paradise, are more complex. Here shallow cavities of var-

The Baptistery floor: dating from the early decades of the 13th century, this replaced the previous crushed brick ("opus signinum") paving, and consists of rectangular marble mosaics designed to look like carpets. The floor's decorative design is more complex and varied in the east area facing the Gates of Paradise, where the ornamentation blends abstract motifs with figures of animals.

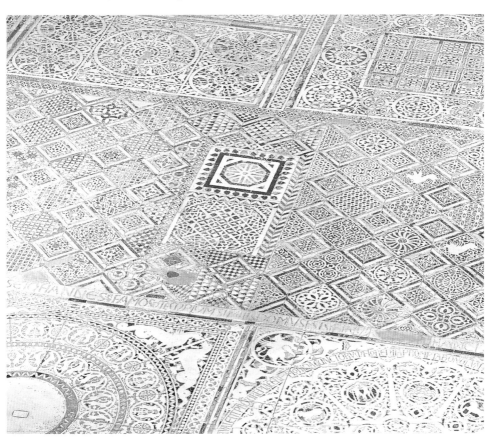

Above: amongst the bichrome inlaid figures decorating the eastern section of the Baptistery floor, we find fabulous creatures, such as the griffon. Below: the signs of the Zodiac, encircled by an inscription in uncial script: "Huc veniant quicumq(ue) volunt miranda videre / Et videant que visa valent pro iure placere / Florida cunctorum Florentia prompta bonorum / Hoc opus implicitum petiit per signa pol[orum] / [...] / [...]ima pavim(en)ti perhibent insigna te(m)plī" (see translation on this page). In earlier times the Zodiac was located near the north portal. According to legend, it was designed by the astronomer Strozzo Strozzi, whose tomb (1052) was discovered in 1351 underneath the east section of the Baptistery. On the strength of this finding, and Giovanni Villani's comment in 1345 ("according to the testimony of old... [the Zodiac] was made for astronomy"), a number of 18th-century scholars, including Giuseppe Richa and Father Ximenes, mistakenly believed the Zodiac to be a gnomon.

ious shapes were gouged out of the white marble slabs paving the floor. The craftsmen then used an iron wire to cut matching shapes out of green serpentine stone, which they set in these recesses, cementing them with lime mortar. This type of inlay is also Roman in origin, and experienced a revival in the 11th century, after Byzantine craftsmen used it to pave the floor of Montecassino Abbey. In Florence another example of the same technique is the floor of the nave at San Miniato al Monte. The year 1207 recorded on it is a precious indication that allows us to establish that similar work in the Baptistery was done in roughly the same period.

The Zodiac

There are indeed many similarities, even in compositional terms, between the floors in these two churches. The Zodiac in the Baptistery actually appears to be derived from the Zodiac in the church of San Miniato. At the end of the marble 'runner', which from the east portal leads to the central area where the baptismal font once stood, we come to a great square containing the wheel of the Zodiac. It is a rose-shaped design marked by twelve colonnettes alternated by medallions enclosing the signs of the Zodiac. At the centre is a corolla that imitates the larger rose shape, and has a radiant sun at its own centre, surrounded by the inscription *En giro torte sol ciclos et rotor igne*, which reads "Behold, I the sun turn the orbits obliquely, and am turned by fire". Another Latin inscription runs along the external edge of the Zodiac wheel, but has some blank spots that make it difficult to translate. It can roughly be rendered thus: "Let all those who wish to be-

hold marvellous things come here, / and let them behold that which, once seen, is indeed capable of pleasing. / Prosperous Florence, abounding in all that's good/ desired this work to be filled with celestial constellations /... / ...The higher things of the sky encircle the lower part of the temple".

An intriguing tradition cited in 1345 in Giovanni Villani's *Cronica* has it that the sun at the centre of the Zodiac was "astronomical" – i.e., that at the summer solstice the ray of sunlight descending from the lantern was supposed to strike it at twelve o' clock noon on the dot. But in fact this phenomenon never occurs. Furthermore, the Zodiac is not equipped with the lines required for a gnomon and other astronomical instruments. It was perhaps only meant to represent the celestial constellations, which were an ornamental motif often used in the 12th and 13th centuries for floors and sculptural work in churches.

Above: the palindrome verse (i.e., reading the same backwards and forwards) placed at the centre of the signs of the Zodiac, encircling the sun: "en giro torte sol ciclos et rotor igne" (translated on p. 52). A similar marble slab may be seen in the church of San Miniato, Florence. Below: Another detail of the Baptistery floor. This section stretches between the baptismal font and the Gates of Paradise, and portrays birds, griffons and lions rampant set inside wheels.

On the entrance side, the Zodiac is preceded by a square of identical shape and size, filled with concentric circles containing a fantastic bestiary. Some scholars consider this be an allusion to the earth. After entering the Baptistery by the main entrance, the faithful would thus follow a symbolic itinerary in three stages: from the bestiary (earthly condition) to the Zodiac, or sky (knowledge of the divine), and finally to the baptismal font (the tangible sign of God's Grace), which at the time was located at the centre of the building.

The 'Carpet' Inlays

The carpet-like inlays flanking the main runner leading to the font also depict lions, griffons and doves – often affronted, in heraldic fashion – alternating each other or entwined with abstract motifs. Both decorative and symbolic, the design of these floor mosaics combine influences of primarily Oriental origin – including Byzantine fabrics and Islamic carvings – which at this time reached Tuscany chiefly through the Republic of Pisa. In this more elaborate section of the Baptistery floor – unfortunately also the most damaged – the green and white marble inlays are enriched with patches of more precious stone, such as red Egyptian porphyry and Greek serpentine, no doubt recovered from Roman sites.

If we wished to date the Baptistery floor section by section, we would have to distinguish between the carpets with simple geometrical patterns (some of these were re-done not so long ago) belonging to the early period, and the more complex inlays near the east door, which draw inspiration from the San Miniato floor (early decades of the 13th century).

Statuary and Other Furnishings in Stone

The Baptismal Font

If we entered the Baptistery through the Gates of Paradise, which for centuries has been the main entrance to the building, and then directed our steps to the wall on

The marble font which still today graces the interior of the Baptistery has an inscription recorded on the reverse side stating that it was commissioned by Arte di Calimala and fashioned in the year 1370. This date rules out Vasari's tentative attribution of the font to Giovanni Pisano. Below: on the south-east side, amongst the scenes of the first order, is St John the Baptist Baptizes Christ. *Opposite page: this 4th-century AD Roman sarcophagus was re-used in 1299 for the burial of Gonfalonier (city magistrate) Guccio de' Medici. The panels depict scenes of a boar hunt, and are meant to extoll the prowess of the deceased. The scene on the front panel is a case in point: the figure of* Virtus, *or* Virtue *(detail above), helps the deceased to aim his spear at the quarry. In the 18th century the sarcophagus was still standing in the Baptistery square, near the walls of Palazzo dei Canonici. In 1824 it was moved to the Medici Riccardi palace, where it remained until the early 1990s.*

the portal's right hand side, we would come to the baptismal font which a Latin inscription at the rear records as having been completed in 1370. It was placed in its present position in 1658, and rests on a base consisting of two steps inlaid with marble. This font remained continuously in use up to the 1970s, when the new custom of baptizing infants in their parish church brought to an end a hoary tradition that had been much cherished by all Florentines.

The font's six faces are carved in high relief and alternated with fascias displaying creepers. The reliefs represent different christenings, and are provided with captions in Latin: *St John Baptizes the Crowds*; *St John Baptizes Christ*; *Christ Baptizes St John*; *Christ Baptizes the Apostles*; *Pope Sylvester the Saint Baptizes Emperor Constantine* and *A Priest Baptizes the Children*. The stories develop a consistent iconographic cycle exemplifying the scriptural foundations of baptism, its effectiveness in history and its central position in the life of the Church. The stylistic features are more difficult to interpret: some authorities detect the work of two different hands here. The last two reliefs appear to be by an artist under the influence of Andrea Orcagna – a major painter and sculptor in Florence at that time – while the more talented author of the other four scenes has a subtlety in modelling and approach that seems to link him to north Italian sculpture. The portions which project more – and where the marble has acquired a transparency akin to alabaster – have been lost over the centuries, and in some cases added on to at a later date. The fine bronze gate enclosing the font also dates from the 14th century, and may have been salvaged from the enclosure of the great baptismal basin demolished in the 16th century.

The Roman Sarcophagi

Two Roman marble sarcophagi stand against the wall connecting the south door to the apse. These coffins were re-used in the 13th century. On the sarcophagus nearest to the entrance we see a crowded hunting scene, which celebrates the deceased, showing him on horseback in the act of hurling a spear at a wild boar. The features of this relief, which is powerfully evocative even in its run-down state, suggest that it dates from the early 4th century AD. The lid was fashioned in 1299, when the sarcophagus was used to entomb the Gonfalonier Guccio de' Medici, a leading official of the Florentine Republic. The top of it is divided into three panels, with the emblem of Arte della Lana, or Wool Guild, and two different versions of the Medici coats of arms in low relief. We have already mentioned that while burial inside the Baptistery was an honour reserved for the lucky few, the area outside the building was dotted with tombs, including many Roman sarcophagi (see p. 12). Guccio's coffin was probably one of them. It must have been shifted often in later centuries, and was finally placed inside the Baptistery in the early 1900s.

The second sarcophagus is of the same provenance. From its style we may presume it to date from the 3rd century AD. In 1230 it was given a new lid and became the coffin of Bishop Giovanni da Velletri. A Latin inscription reads: "Velletri was the homeland of the Blessed Bishop Giovanni, who lies (here). May he rest in peace". The symbolic scene carved on the front of the sarcophagus is obscure. The coffin may once have contained the remains of a woman. She is depicted at the centre of the relief, in the act of offering a small casket.

Right: St John the Baptist. *This image was sculpted by Giuseppe Piamontini and presented to the Baptistery by Grand Duke Cosimo III. In the early years it stood on the altar dedicated to Florence's patron Saint. Below: the Romanesque altar seen from the front. It was reconstructed in the early 1900s, following drawings which Anton Francesco Gori, a provost of the Baptistery, made of it prior to its destruction in 1731. It served as a model for the altar in the Old Sacristy in the church of San Lorenzo, and for the St Zenobius altar in Florence Cathedral. It is cited by Boccaccio in a passage of the Decameron, where Calandrino is "carefully studying the paintings and carving on the tabernacle which stands on top of the altar" (VIII,3). Opposite page: a candelabrum which is thought to have been employed for Easter rites. On the plinth at the base of the colonnette is an inscription reading: "Johannes Jacobi de Florentia me fecit A.D. MCCCXX" (John, son of Jacob the Florentine, fashioned me in 1320). Scholars believe that both the date and the signature refer only to the bas-reliefs on the column.*

Piamontini's St John the Baptist

Between the two sarcophagi described above, is to be found a marble statue of St John the Baptist by Giovanni Piamontini (1664-1742). The ultra-pious Grand Duke Cosimo III donated it to the Baptistery in 1688. Originally it was on the altar dedicated to St John the Baptist, which stands against the wall behind the 1370 baptismal font, and is opposite the altar of the Virgin Mary and the altar of the Crucifix. All three furnishings were removed during the 1898-1908 restoration program, which eliminated all Baroque additions. Deprived of the majestic canopy above it, Piamontini's finely designed and modelled statue today looks very much out of place.

The Altar in the Apse

The altar that is now in the *scarsella* was re-assembled in the early 1900s, in an effort to restore the interior of the Baptistery to its original Romanesque appearance. The altar, which in the first half of the 14th century included a painted tabernacle, was dismantled in 1731 to make way for Girolamo Ticciati's monumental late Baroque altar. Its destruction was deplored by many a cultured Florentine of those times. Anton Francesco Gori preserved many marble sections, as well as a series of drawings which at the beginning of the 20th century enabled the architect Giovanni Castellucci to fashion a credible imitation of it. The altar's long sides are divided into three compartments with inlays. At the centre is a recess for the display of relics (*confessio*). Stylistically similar to the Baptistery's interior, the altar was probably made sometime between the late 1100s and early 1200s.

The Paschal Candelabrum

To the right of the altar in the apse is a paschal candelabrum in white and green marble. Nearly three metres in height, it consists of a pedestal, a lion bearing a column decorated with historical scenes, topped by an angel holding a candlestick. These four elements were thought by some to be of different origin, and to have been assem-

bled at a later date. Nevertheless, the lion is present in many candelabra of the Romanesque period, and the column with reliefs of angels, prophets, doctors of the Church and Evangelists clearly expresses the symbolism of salvation and resurrection associated with Easter celebrations. The date 1320 is inscribed at the foot of the candelabrum, as well as the author's name, one Giovanni di Giacomo da Firenze. The column and the angel might be by another artist, even though the style suggests that both sections of the object date from the same period.

The Sarcophagus of Bishop Ranieri

The sarcophagus of Bishop Ranieri stands against the wall, to the right of the *scarsella*, and contains the body of Bishop Ranieri (died 12 July, 1113). The white marble parallelepiped, decorated with simple squares of green marble, resembles the same bichrome scheme of the building's interior, indicating that it probably is of a later date. On the front is a long Latin inscription commemorating this cleric, who was Bishop of Florence for 42 long years, "a good and just man, wise and of pleasing appearance".

The Tomb of Antipope John XXIII

After Bishop Ranieri's entombment – and perhaps still in the 12th century – burial inside the Baptistery was strictly forbidden. Early in the next century Florence's Podestà, or chief magistrate, Bonifacio Lupi, so desired to be buried here that he offered to finance further mosaic decoration of the dome. His request, however, met with a flat refusal. Towards the middle of the following century, under the rule of Cosimo the Elder, this unusual honour was granted to Cardinal Baldassarre Cossa, a figure closely linked to the Medici family. Cossa came from a noble Neapolitan family, and had become personally involved in the Great Schism. This was one of the Church's darkest and most troubled periods, a time when three men claimed the title of pope, the first in Avignon, the second in Rome and the third in Pisa. Cossa became the second 'Pisan' pope, taking the name of John XXIII. In 1415 the Council of Constance deposed him as well as the other two popes, Benedict XIII in Avignon, and the 'Roman' Gregory XII. Two years later the Council put a final end to the rift by installing in Rome a fourth pope, Martin V. After recognizing this pontiff's authority, Cossa retired to private life in Florence, where he died in 1419. It was probably to secure the privilege of being buried in the Baptistery, that Cossa published his last will in his lifetime. This included large donations to the Baptistery. In 1422 the Cardinal's executors – Cosimo the Elder amongst them – were authorized to erect the sepulchre Cossa had so longed for. Under the terms of the official document granting this permission, the monument had to be "short and exceedingly reasonable, so as not to occupy the entrance of the church, for the honour of being buried here is no small thing; and let this suffice".

Baldassarre Cossa's funeral monument is wedged in between the two columns which stand beside the sarcophagus of Bishop Ranieri. Its execution was entrusted to Donatello, who probably started work

This funeral monument, designed by Donatello and executed by him in association with Michelozzo, commemorates Baldassarre Cossa, the Antipope John XXIII. On the sarcophagus is the inscription: "Ioa(n)nes quo(n)dam papa / XIII° obiit Florentie a/n(n)o D(omi)ni MCCCCXVIIII XI / kalendas ianuarii". In vain did Pope Martin V – who had appointed Cossa Bishop of Frascati – press the Florentine authorities to refer to him simply as "Neapolitanus cardinalis". A deeply original example of a funeral monument, this work has been the object of passionate debate amongst art historians, especially as regards the extent of the contribution given to its execution by Michelozzo, who is known to have joined Donatello's workshop in 1425.

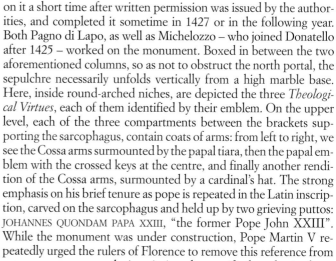

on it a short time after written permission was issued by the authorities, and completed it sometime in 1427 or in the following year. Both Pagno di Lapo, as well as Michelozzo – who joined Donatello after 1425 – worked on the monument. Boxed in between the two aforementioned columns, so as not to obstruct the north portal, the sepulchre necessarily unfolds vertically from a high marble base. Here, inside round-arched niches, are depicted the three *Theological Virtues*, each of them identified by their emblem. On the upper level, each of the three compartments between the brackets supporting the sarcophagus, contain coats of arms: from left to right, we see the Cossa arms surmounted by the papal tiara, then the papal emblem with the crossed keys at the centre, and finally another rendition of the Cossa arms, surmounted by a cardinal's hat. The strong emphasis on his brief tenure as pope is repeated in the Latin inscription, carved on the sarcophagus and held up by two grieving puttos: JOHANNES QUONDAM PAPA XXIII, "the former Pope John XXIII". While the monument was under construction, Pope Martin V repeatedly urged the rulers of Florence to remove this reference from the inscription, the pontifical seat having been unlawfully claimed by Cardinal Cossa. The gilt bronze figure of the deceased, enveloped in a bishop's vestments, lies on a funeral bed surmounted by a marble canopy. The canopy's underside is decorated with red and blue ramages, reminiscent of the ornate fabrics of the period and made by filling with coloured wax the motif carved into the marble.

Although he was assisted by others – including his partner Michelozzo, who probably did the marble relief of the *Virgin Mary with Child* above the image of the deceased – this innovative work is unquestionably Donatello's own. The artist emphasizes the human and temporal aspect of death, playing down the religious side, which had up to then been the fundamental to all funerary art. While the allegorical figures on the base and the sorrowing puttos – the latter derived from ancient Roman models – follow more traditional compositional criteria, the illusionistic canopy is an entirely novel idea, which. opens dramatically on the funeral chamber, where the deceased is depicted with strong naturalism lying on his deathbed. The intensity of this representation is increased by the chromatic contrast between the dusky-hued bronze pall and the burnished gilt bronze image of the deceased. This effect had been partially lost due to a dark varnish perhaps added late in the 18th century, which lent the same dull shade to both. Opificio's restorers removed it in 1986.

Left: detail of the Theological Virtues, *carved on the base of the monument. They stand inside shells which repeat the motif of the lunette overhead. As much as Donatello's style can be detected in all these figures, some scholars believe that only the bronze statue of the deceased was actually carved by him. The statue's gilding was recently restored to its original brilliance. Below: these wall paintings imitating marble inlays adorn one of the coretti inside the women's gallery, on the south-east side of the building. They date from the 13th century.*

Wall Paintings

Between the ground floor – which in the past was richer in monumental furnishings – and the golden mosaics spreading across the Baptistery's pavilion-shaped dome, is the women's gallery. This runs along seven sides of the building. Light enters each section through the mullioned windows with two lights opening on the interior of the building. In the early 14th century, four such sections, or coretti, were covered with mosaics (see p. 102). In earlier times, however, the walls and vaults of all twenty-one sections (three to each side) were decorated with painted green-and-white designs imitating the marble inlays elsewhere in the building. During the thorough restoration program launched at the end of the 19th century to restore the Baptistery to its original appearance, the wall paintings resurfaced, albeit with some gaps, from under the many layers of whitewash which in the past had almost entirely blotted them out.

The artistic medium devised for the *loggetta* of the women's gallery does not, as we have just seen, follow the illustrative type of program so common in churches' interiors, but portrays abstract and symbolic figures. This choice appears to be part of a conscious effort to harmonize the Baptistery's decorative scheme with its general architectural scheme. Although there is no written record to tell us exactly when the decorative cycle of mural paintings in the gallery was undertaken, it is safe to assume that they date from the 13th century.

As we move from section to section, we find that the subjects depicted here include interlacing arabesques and images of animals portrayed in the expressive, concise and strongly naturalistic manner that first appeared in geometric inlay work at about that time. Certain liturgical objects portrayed here, such as the processional cross with the transverse beam ending in trefoils, a Gothic-style clasp and several candelabra, were probably done even later. One of the latter is modelled on the archaic candle holders portrayed on the inlays on the triumphal arch in the church of San Miniato al Monte, while others are jointed and slim like the candelabra used in churches in the sec-

Opposite page: the first, or uppermost, register (i.e. horizontal zone) of the mosaics decorating the vault of the dome. This area surrounding the base of the lantern was the most damaged over the centuries by infiltration of rainwater. The mosaics here have been so heavily retouched that only one of the sixteen heads depicted in the eight segments – the one between pairs of affronted porpoises and animals at a spring (including deer, peacocks, buffaloes, quail, oxen, hens, rams and cranes) – can be said to be authentic 13th-century work.

ond half of the 13th century. Some animals and such objects as the bowls and vases – whose symbolic value did not prevent the artists from portraying them in an animated and light-hearted manner – appear to be derived from similar shapes depicted in the marble inlays situated above the gallery. Others – such as the pair of interlaced dolphins, birds flanking a vase and forked creepers sprouting out of vases – are probably modelled on the mosaics surrounding the lantern and in the *scarsella*. This gives us additional evidence pointing to a conscious plan to unify the decoration in the Baptistery's interior. It is safe to assume, then, that the great mosaic cycle on the dome was either started earlier than these mural paintings, or that the two were launched at roughly the same time. After completion of the mosaics, the dimly lit coretti in the women's gallery would indeed have remained the only visible part on the elevation of the Baptistery's interior to remain without decoration.

The differences in style and execution in the mural paintings which decorate the women's gallery lead us to conjecture that different artists may have worked on them at different times. We do note, however, that in spite of this fact, the cycle does not seem to show a definite stylistic and chronological development – as do, for example, the mosaics in the women's gallery. The bichrome colour scheme (achieved with a black pigment derived from the bryony plant, and the marble-hued 'San Giovanni' white paint), as well as the free-hand execution, without use of stencils, are common to all the sections of the gallery. This explains the freshness of the images, but also the occasional rough and careless treatment of much of the ornamental detail.

That several artists contributed to the murals in the gallery is further suggested by some of the many graffiti scratched into the plaster. These inscriptions are a significant example of anecdotal history, and testify to the fact that these rooms were in use from the earliest times, both for maintenance purposes and liturgical reasons. While some of the inscriptions appear to have been made by individuals who wished to consign their names to posterity, others refer directly to the work force employed in the Baptistery. A 15th-century inscription tells us of the leave of absence taken by a workman named Meo: "Meo left on 25 June 1477, and came back here on 7 September 1480". On the south and south-east walls, the graffiti go back to an earlier period. We find two dates recorded, 1308 and 1334, together with the names Piero, Chalandrino, Lapo and Salvino. These are followed by a succession of vertical lines, and may well be a reference to the number of work days completed by each. The section of the gallery to the right of the *scarsella* contains several graffiti dating from the 15th century, which rather immodestly list the names of the clerics who probably used this area as a singing gallery.

The Mosaics

After marvelling at the choice marbles that pave the ground and panel the walls of the Baptistery, we look up and realize that the mosaics overhead are the crowning glory of all this decorative effort.

Like a sky glittering with gold and a wealth of colours, the mosaics cover the lofty dome, and from there spread to its drum-shaped base, to the apse's arch and vaulted ceiling, to the parapets and inner sections of the women's gallery, and finally to the lintels spanning the doors.

Even though new mosaics were added in the early decades of the 14th century (with a brief spurt of activity coming as late as the 1400s), the main bulk of this extraordinary artistic undertaking was conceived and executed in the 13th century, and made possible by Florence's rise to economic and artistic prominence. The necessary financial resources probably became available after the 1216 agreement between Opera of San Giovanni and the wealthy Arte di Calimala. From that year on – and for centuries to come – the guild held the patronage of the Baptistery and financed all the decorative programs destined for it.

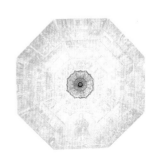

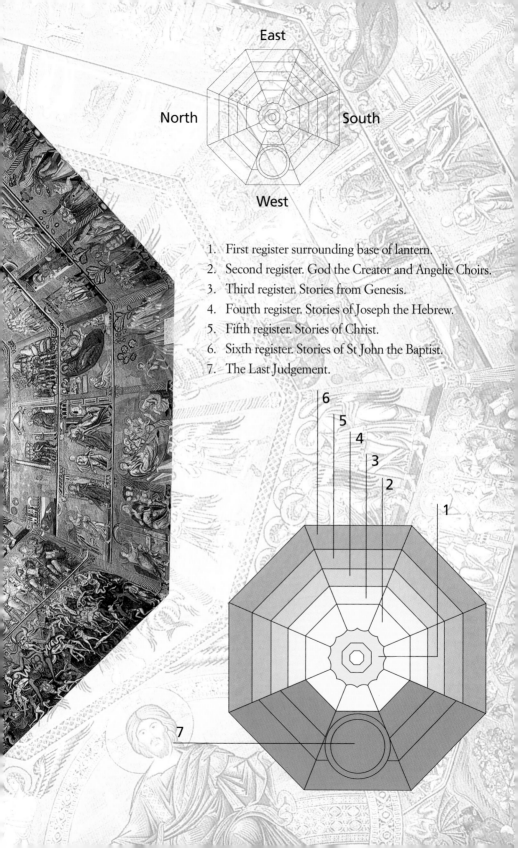

East

North

South

West

1. First register surrounding base of lantern.
2. Second register. God the Creator and Angelic Choirs.
3. Third register. Stories from Genesis.
4. Fourth register. Stories of Joseph the Hebrew.
5. Fifth register. Stories of Christ.
6. Sixth register. Stories of St John the Baptist.
7. The Last Judgement.

The second register of the mosaics on the dome depicts the Almighty Father *and the* Heavenly Hosts. *Here, too – like in the case of the untouched head in the uppermost register (see above) – scholars have detected a stylistic similarity with the Lucca artist Bonaventura Berlinghieri. This connection is all the more meaningful if we think that the decoration on the façade of the church of San Frediano at Lucca is a tangible proof of the spread of mosaic decoration in 13th century western Tuscany.*

The merchants' guild undertook to engage 'maestri musivarii', or artists expert in setting mosaics – an art hitherto unpractised in Florence – and to purchase the precious polychrome and gold enamels, which are the raw materials from which mosaic tesserae are made. The organizers realized that, due to its complexity, the program would take much longer to complete than a cycle of wall paintings, the decorative medium usually used in those times.

The artists prepared a preliminary drawing on a cartoon, which probably included an accurate plotting of the background colours as well. From this model, the sinopia was roughly sketched in red on the first layer of plaster, or *arriccio.* A second layer of mortar was then applied to the wall – in sections that could be completed in the space of one day – and into this were embedded the tiny mosaic particles. Thus, piece by piece, and in accordance with a complex overall design, the images took shape on the wall. Mosaic particles were obtained from discs of vitreous paste produced in specialized kilns in the Republic of Venice. A workman struck these with a hammer, and then pared each single piece by hand to the required shape and size.

First and foremost, Florence dedicated this masterpiece – an unprecedented accomplishment even for the rich and cultured Tuscany – "to the greater glory of God" (*ad maiorem Dei gloriam*). But the mosaics were also meant to demonstrate the city's supremacy over its rivals, and underscore the spirit of the inscription on the floor of the Baptistery (see p. 52), which calls on all visitors to admire the wonders in this building and in this town which, is "Prosperous [and] abounding in all that's good", and can thus accomplish a feat of this magnitude.

Only a handful of fragmentary documents survive to record a decorative program, which took seventy-five years to complete. These go from 1271, when work was already underway, to 1325, when the mosaics in the areas below the dome were nearing completion, but disappointingly give us the names of only three contributing artists, who probably succeeded each other on the site. The first is one Francesco, a "master mosaicist" probably of Pisan origin, who was dismissed in 1298, and immediately thereafter started work on the mosaics on the bowl-shaped vault of the apse of Pisa Cathedral (later completed by Cimabue). The other two, Bingo and Pazzo, were also relieved of their duties in the early years of the 14th century, after being charged with stealing mosaic pieces. For his part, Vasari cites two mosaicists, Andrea Tafi and Gaddo Gaddi, both native Florentines. The latter appears to have been an assistant of Giotto's, who is also known to have tried his hand at this art. However, given the total absence of works that can be safely attributed to either one of these two artists, we may only guess what sections of the mosaics, if any, were done by them. This leaves us with a tentative stylistic analysis, which is further jeopardized by the numerous and often misleading restoration programs of later ages.

The Mosaics on the Dome

In examining the mosaics in the Baptistery, we shall not follow their physical distribution inside the building, but their chronological sequence. Let us start with the dome's pavilion-shaped interior.

All eight segments of the dome (matching the Baptistery's eight outer walls) are covered with mosaics. They are divided into six superimposed horizontal zones, or registers, covering an area of more than 100 square metres. At the summit, the register encircling the base of the lantern is pavilion-shaped and has sixteen concave sides. Here we have symbolic and ornamental themes: dolphins, acanthus ornament, heads inside medallions, and different kinds of animals in pairs drinking at a spring. The second register is divided by mosaicked columns into eight segments depicting the *Creator* and the nine *Angelic Choirs*. Next to the full-length figure of the blessing *Creator*, who with his left hand holds an open book with the inscription CREAVI DEUS ANGELOS, we see pairs of *Cherubim* and *Seraphim*. The seven other ranks of angelic beings occupy the other segments. They are: *Dominions, Powers, Archangels, Angels, Principalities, Virtues* and *Thrones*. Each choir is represented by a pair of angels.

In the four lower registers, the three segments above the *scarsella* are occupied by the *Last Judgement*. In the central segment we see the imposing figure of *Christ the Judge* inside an almond-shaped kernel of light. Directly below, the elect and the wicked are seen rising out of the sepulchre. In the two segments flanking the Christ, the composition unfolds symmetrically across three registers. In the upper register two processions of angels bearing the symbols of Christ's Passion, preceded by two angels blowing the trumpets of God, approach the Saviour. In the middle register, the twelve *Apostles*, the *Virgin Mary* and *St John the Baptist* are seated on thrones on either side of Christ. In the lower register are the elect who have gathered to adore Christ,

Mosaics on the Baptistery dome, second register, east segment. Authored by an artist working under the influence of Bonaventura Berlinghieri, this section of the mosaics was completed between 1240 and 1250 and portrays the Almighty *God raising his hand in blessing, surrounded by Cherubim and Seraphim. In his left hand the Father holds an open book containing the words, "Creavi Deus Angelos" ("I created the Angels"). At either side of the Almighty's halo are the first and last letters of the Greek alphabet, Alpha and Omega. The Omega has probably been vitiated by over-restoration.*

and *Paradise*, where the patriarchs *Abraham, Isaac* and *Jacob* are seated holding the elect on their knees. To the right, the vision of *Hell* is dominated by Lucifer, a horrifying figure who grabs and devours the damned. The latter are also the victims of different tortures inflicted upon them by demons.

To the right of the *Last Judgement*, starting from the third register, we see four different series of narratives: *Stories from Genesis, Stories of Joseph the Hebrew, Stories of Christ* and *Stories of St John the Baptist*. These extend across five segments, on four superimposed registers. Each register includes three scenes divided by columns. In each segment we thus find twelve scenes, except for the fifth and last segment (to the left of the *Last Judgement*), which has eleven stories, since the upper register – *Stories from Genesis* – is divided into two scenes only. Each narrative sequence, then, moves from one segment to the following on the same level, and reaches a total of fifteen scenes – except for *Genesis*, which has fourteen.

Restoration Programs

Over the centuries the mosaics on the Baptistery dome have undergone many restoration programs, some of which can hardly be detected. The first of these got underway as early as the 14th century, while the last major job was carried out by Opificio delle Pietre Dure between 1898 and 1907. Rainwater has proved to be one of the mosaics' most insidious enemies. Leaking through the roof of the dome, it had already begun to do damage in the early 1300s. Restoration campaigns are known to have been launched in 1384, 1402, 1483-1490, 1781-1782, and 1820-1823. In the late 15th century Alessio Baldovinetti, a well-known expert in mosaic techniques, was appointed supervisor of a laborious refurbishing program. After him the art of mosaic setting in Florence disappeared very quickly. In the 18th and 19th centuries the large gaps in the mosaics were filled with scenes painted on plaster. During the last important refurbishing, in the late 1800s, Opificio's expert mosaic restorers removed all the portions

painted on plaster, and patched them with glass tesserae especially produced in Venetian kilns for this purpose. No effort was spared to imitate the original style. On this occasion, *Lamech Kills Cain* and two stories of the *Ark of Noah*, which had long before deteriorated beyond recognition and been replaced with plaster paintings, were entirely reset in mosaic after cartoons prepared by the painter Arturo Viligiardi. The job is cited in an inscription extending across the three scenes and bearing the date 1906.

Chronology and Style of the Mosaics on the Dome

A proper historical and artistic analysis of the mosaics of the Baptistery dome is rendered difficult by the sections lost over the ages and by later restoration programs. A paucity of documents recording its execution further complicates matters. The few relevant contemporary accounts are: 1) a 1271 agreement, whereby Arte di Calimala undertook to finance the program; 2) records of a further subsidy made in 1281; 3) the abovementioned dismissal of three craftsmen; 4) a final document, dated 1325, pertaining to fresh subsidies for the portions of mosaic being completed in the areas below the dome.

Given the lack of reliable information, the chronology of these mosaics and the identity of its creators both remain open to debate. Opinions also differ widely on the actual stages of execution. Some believe the work proceeded segment by segment, starting from the lower registers and working up to the higher ones. Indeed, the technique of mosaic setting does not require a fixed sequence, as does fresco painting, where work must necessarily progress from the higher registers to the lower ones. But a stylistic study of the mosaics of the dome leads us to believe that work started in the upper portion of the dome, and then continued on the lower level, where we see *God the Creator* and the *Angelic Choirs*. After this register was finished, the circular progression of work round the dome appears to have stopped, probably because the scaffolding required for this would have occu-

Mosaics on the Baptistery dome, second register, north-west segment: the Dominions, *one of the Angelic ranks. Executed by a Florentine artist, probably between 1250 and 1260.*

Mosaics on the Baptistery dome, second register, north and north-east segments: attributed to the Master of Santa Maria Primerana, the Powers *(ca. 1250-1260?) wear a lorica and helmet, and grasp a sword, spear and shield. The* Archangels *holding a scroll with the words "Animadvertes" date from the same period, but have been more generically ascribed to a Florentine artist.*

pied all the available room inside the Baptistery, leaving none at all for the many religious and civil ceremonies regularly held here. Work then proceeded segment by segment, always moving from the upper levels to the lower ones. After completion of the three segments devoted to the *Last Judgement* (whose style suggests it was done right after the *Angelic Choirs*), came the *Stories*, starting with the segment on the right hand side of the *Last Judgement*. In the sequence of segments in clockwise order and registers from top to bottom, we find only one discrepancy, consisting of the second and third stories of the cycle *Joseph the Hebrew*. Although physically adjacent and chronologically contemporary to the *Last Judgement*, both these scenes appear to be by the same later artist who authored the final sections of the mosaics on the Baptistery dome.

The execution of the cycle can be tentatively placed somewhere between 1240 and 1310. This is true at least for the stylistic features of the pictorial models. The actual setting of the mosaics may well have taken longer.

Given the sheer scope and duration of the undertaking, there is no doubt that a good number of artists and mosaicists took part in it, even though the overall iconographic scheme and compositional structure of the program – with its sturdy framework of columns breaking up the stories on the different levels – had certainly been finalized before the work actually started.

Scholars generally incline to the view that the mosaicists who worked on the Baptistery dome came mostly from other Italian cities, particularly from Venice, which at that time was a major producer of mosaics. Although new to the city of Florence, other Tuscan cities, such as Pisa and Lucca, were artistically far advanced in this field, having already launched mosaic programs in the early 13th century. It is perhaps no coincidence that near the dome's summit there is a head (untouched by later alterations) that reminds us of the pictorial style then in vogue in Lucca, and especially of the work of Bonaventura Berlinghieri. In the register which immediately follows this one – both in terms of position and probable date of execution – and portrays *God the Creator and the Angelic Choirs*, we again detect the same influence, which permeated Florentine painting in or shortly after the mid 1200s. Indeed, to understand the stylistic features and evolution of the mosaics on the dome, we must necessarily go back to Florentine painting. Whatever the origin of the craftsmen who stood atop the scaffolding, deftly embedding glass tesserae in the fresh plaster, the men who designed the cartoons – an indispensable first step leading to the finished product – assuredly were Florentine – or at any rate Tuscan – painters active in the second half of the 13th century, a period teeming with artists who shaped artistic trends immediately before Giotto's stylistic revolution.

Coppo di Marcovaldo and Meliore, both of them central figures in Florentine painting before Cimabue, may be credited with the majestic scene depicted in the *Last Judgement*, while the two upper friezes in the adjacent register appear to have been designed by the author of the highly figurative *Hell*, which has a stylistic affinity to Coppo's work. In the third register of this same segment, which contains a series of *Stories of Jesus Christ* (much altered by later restora-

Mosaics on the Baptistery dome, second register, east segment: the Angels *here may date from 1250-1260, and have been attributed to the Master of Santa Maria Primerana.*

tion), we meet another artist, whose style recalls a number of Byzantine-style paintings – such as the *Madonna Enthroned*, in the nearby church of Santa Maria Maggiore – done before Cimabue.

Cimabue's influence is evident on the author who completed this first segment of the *Stories* in the fourth register, and also worked on the two upper registers of the second segment. This is particularly noticeable in the figures' forceful, strongly marked facial traits.

The second segment also points to the contribution of a third artist – or perhaps a full-fledged workshop – linked to the prolific Master of Mary Magdalen. In the Baptistery dome this artist is responsible for the greatest number of mosaics, including the second segment and the entire third segment, as well as the two upper registers of the fourth segment – thus a total of twenty-three scenes. The subtle stylistic variations that are noticeable in them are probably due to the presence of several artists in the same workshop. In any case, they are modelled on the greatest pictorial works of the 13th century (from Cimabue down to the Sienese painter Duccio di Boninsegna) and use a language that is attractive and strongly illustrative, a fact that explains why this workshop was so popular in Florence during the last two decades of the 1200s.

In the two lower registers of the fourth segment, a new and significant artist makes his appearance. Some authorities have believed this to be Gaddo Gaddi. Gaddi was a friend of Giotto's and father to Taddeo, one of the master's most talented disciples. Although Vasari mentions Gaddo Gaddi in his *Lives*, we must remember that this biographer was often off the mark when recording events that took place long before his time. Gaddi's artistic personality is in fact too indefinite for us to safely attribute any work to him, whether in the Baptistery or anywhere else. But the author of these two registers can also be credited with the mosaic lunette (the *Coronation of the Virgin Mary*) on the counter-façade of Santa Maria del Fiore, although this work is probably earlier. While here the influence of Cimabue appears to be more marked, the majestic stories of Christ and St John in the Baptistery suggest that this anonymous artist's initial Tuscan style matured when he came into contact with the Roman artists who worked on the Basilica of Assisi during the period prior to Giotto's involvement. Their influence certainly seems to weigh on the monumental scale and on the naturalistic and classicizing treatment of the figures in such scenes as the *Capture of Christ*, or *St John the Baptist Sends His Disciples to Christ*. But there is also an expressive and impassioned manner in rendering the stories that specifically recalls the great Giotto himself.

The artist of the next two higher registers of the last segment also seems to have imbibed the lessons of the painters of Assisi Cathedral. Let us remember that the Assisi workshop was the most decisive influence on Italian painting in the last quarter of the 13th century. He appears to be equally familiar with the innovations of the fresco cycle depicting the *Stories of St Francis*, which Giotto did in the upper basilica. The further development of Giotto's painting is basic to the language employed in the third register. Here the *Crucifixion* is entirely overshadowed by a dramatically realistic portrayal of the dead Christ, which draws from Giotto's revolutionary rendition of this scene on the painted tableau for the church of Santa Maria Novella.

Mosaics on the Baptistery dome, second register, south-east, south and south-west segments: probably authored by a Florentine artist working between 1250 and 1260, the angels of Principalities *grasp a Crusader's banner, while the* Virtues *are shown in the act of freeing man from Satan. The angels of* Thrones *– believed by scholars to have been executed between 1240 and 1250 by the* Master of San Francesco Bardi *– hold up the almond-shaped kernel, which in the Byzantine tradition is a symbol of the divine throne.*

Opposite page: the Last Judgement *takes up all the three lower registers in the south-west, west and north-west segments of the dome. Executed between 1260 and 1275, it includes a round zone of no less than eight metres in diameter, containing* Christ the Judge. *This mosaic has been attributed to a follower of Meliore, himself a forerunner of Cimabue's. Left, starting from the top: the upper register traversing the north-west and south-west segments depicts* Angels with the trumpets of God and the symbols of the Passion *(1260-1270); in the lower register, the same segments – probably decorated by members of Meliore's entourage – represent the* Madonna, Angels and Apostles *(south-west segment) and* St John the Baptist, Angels and Apostles *(south-east segment). Mary and St John are thus cast in the role of intercessors pleading on behalf of mankind before Christ the Judge. As some scholars have pointed out, the placing of the angels here is rather unusual, as they are usually depicted standing beside the souls of the resurrected.*

The mosaics in the last register of the three segments above the scarsella were done between 1260 and 1275 by followers of Coppo di Marcovaldo and Meliore, who here portrayed the Elect in Paradise, *and the* Damned in Hell. *The decidedly grim representation of the damned not only includes Judas the Traitor still dangling from the tree where he hanged himself after betraying Christ, but potentates and clerics as well. Hellfire has also engulfed a monk in a black habit, who probably belongs to the Benedictine Order. This is an intriguing addition, because all the other representatives of the new Orders working in Florence at that time – including Franciscans and Dominicans – have been put amongst the Elect.*

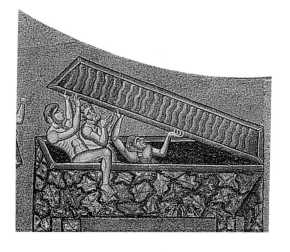

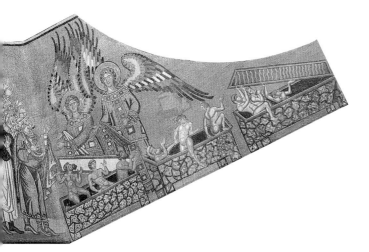

More unassuming and conversational in tone, although not entirely lacking in elegance, is the author who in the early 1300s completed the fourth register, and thus the covering of the dome, with a number of *Stories of St John the Baptist*.

Story Cycles in the Mosaics on the Dome

Stories from Genesis

The four series of sacred stories start in the segment on the right hand side of the *Last Judgement*, and progress in clockwise fashion across five segments. Each cycle of stories is assigned to one register. To follow its development we must follow the same register extending across five segments. The upper register – the third from the top – consists of fourteen scenes devoted to the events narrated in Genesis, for it is upon the first book of the Scriptures that the monumental construction of Christian thought has been erected.

1a. *Creation of the World* (north segment). The Almighty appears inside a starry hemisphere. Below is the creation, represented by the sun, the moon, the creatures of the air, the earth and the water, and Adam and Eve. Often retouched. Probably by an artist close to Coppo di Marcovaldo. Ca. 1270-1275.

2a. *Creation of Adam* (north segment). The Almighty is shown in the Garden of Eden, seated on a globe, in the act of bringing Adam to life. Almost entirely redone in the late 19th century. Situated in the sequence attributed to Coppo's entourage, this is presumably his work.

Mosaics on the Baptistery dome, third register, north and north-east segments: The first scenes of the Stories from Genesis *start from the* Creation *(opposite page, below: a detail of the* Creation of Eve, *by an artist associated with Coppo di Marcovaldo). The narration continues with episodes linked to the theme of original sin, and reaches its climax with the* Expulsion from the Garden of Eden *(opposite page, above), executed between 1280 and 1285 by an artist influenced by Cimabue. Before the 20th-century restoration the figures of Adam and Eve were patchy, while the cherub was almost entirely painted on plaster.*

3a. *Creation of Eve* (north segment). While Adam is fast asleep, the Almighty causes Eve to spring out of his body. The three scenes in the upper register of this segment have been heavily altered. Nevertheless, this scene contains more original parts than the others, notably in the figures of Adam and Eve. The sleeping Adam resembles the hanged *Judas* in the adjacent scene of *Hell*. By an artist of Coppo's entourage. Ca. 1270-1275.

4a. *The Original Sin* (north-east segment). Urged on by the snake, Adam and Eve pick fruits from the forbidden tree. The mosaic in its present form is almost entirely the result of late-19th-century restoration, thus ruling out a stylistic analysis. This scene is presumably also by the artist of the Cimabue school who worked at other scenes in this segment.

5a. *Adam and Eve are Reproached by the Almighty* (north-east segment). Adam and Eve, now conscious and ashamed of their nudity, are cursed by the Almighty for their disobedience. The entire figure of the Almighty was redone during the 1898-1908 restoration program, while the heads of Adam and Eve – in particular the sturdy and strongly outlined features of the latter – retain the stamp given them by the artist, who is stylistically akin to Cimabue. Ca. 1280-1285.

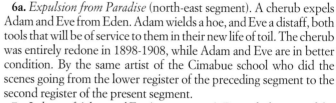

Mosaics on the Baptistery dome, third register, east and south-east segments: the Stories from Genesis continue with the Labour of Adam and Eve, and the events affecting their children Cain and Abel. This is followed by a scene in which God calls Noah before the Flood.

6a. *Expulsion from Paradise* (north-east segment). A cherub expels Adam and Eve from Eden. Adam wields a hoe, and Eve a distaff, both tools that will be of service to them in their new life of toil. The cherub was entirely redone in 1898-1908, while Adam and Eve are in better condition. By the same artist of the Cimabue school who did the scenes going from the lower register of the preceding segment to the second register of the present segment.

7a. *Labour of Adam and Eve* (east segment). Beneath the gaze of the Almighty, Adam and Eve, dressed in animal skins, do their work. Eve spins, while her husband ploughs the soil. This scene is in fairly good condition, in spite of its having been retouched a number of times. By an artist of the Cimabue school, less forceful than the author of the preceding segment, and partial to the milder manner typical of the prolific workshop of the Master of Mary Magdalen. Ca. 1280-1290.

8a. *Cain and Abel* (east segment). The two brothers offer the fruit of their labour to God. Cain lays the harvest on the altar, while Abel offers a lamb, blessed by the hand of the Lord. This scene has been heavily restored, and cannot be reliably evaluated. Probably by the artist who did the preceding scene and the register running immediately below.

9a. *Cain kills Abel* (east segment). The slain Abel lies at the feet of Cain, who still holds the stick in his hand as he hearkens to the Almighty's curse. The right-hand section of this scene was restored in 1898-1908. The other sections are equally impaired. Probably by the same artist who did the three higher registers in this segment, and who belonged to the workshop of the Master of Mary Magdalen.

10a. *Lamech Kills Cain* (south-east segment). The old and nearly blind Lamech, a descendant of Cain, goes hunting with his son Tubal-kain. He sees Cain in the undergrowth, mistakes him for his quarry and fells him with an arrow. The three scenes of the upper register of this segment (the fourth segment in clockwise direction starting from the *Last Judgement*) having been lost, the painter Luigi Ademollo filled the gaps with paintings on plaster between 1820 and 1823. These were later removed and once again mosaicked, following cartoons prepared by the painter Arturo Viligiardi. His name and the date of execution, 1906, are recorded in an inscription spanning the three scenes.

11a. *God Commands Noah to Build the Ark* (south-east segment). Accompanied by his three sons Sem, Cam and Japhet, Noah receives

Mosaics on the Baptistery dome, third register, south-east segment: The Construction of the Ark: *this was one of the scenes reconstructed by Arturo Viligiardi in 1906, to replace portions of the mosaic which had been irreparably damaged.*

Mosaics on the Baptistery dome, third register, south segment: done in the 1290s by an artist working in the Sienese style, this depiction of the Entry into the Ark *(detail shown on the right) occupies an area twice the size of the others, for in fact it represents two distinct episodes: the animals enter into the Ark first, and are then followed by Noah and his family. Below: the south segment of the third register: the* Stories from Genesis *end with this depiction of* The Flood.

God's order to build the Ark. Like the scenes preceding and following it in the same register, this one was redone in 1906 from a cartoon by Arturo Viligiardi.

12a. *Construction of the Ark* (south-east segment). Noah oversees his sons' construction of a large ark in which they will ride the floodwaters. Done in 1906 to replace fallen portions.

13a-14a. *Noah Enters the Ark* (south segment). Still following the divine Will, Noah boards the Ark with his wife, three sons, daughters-in-law, and the different animals in pairs. This is the only case in the cycle of scriptural stories depicted on the Baptistery dome in which a single scene occupies an area normally meant for two. In actual fact, this scene merges two episodes in the story: 1) the animals and 2) Noah's family boarding the Ark. Earlier iconographic cycles presented the two episodes separately. In spite of much restoration, the mosaic is fairly authentic, at least the part with the figures. The work of a skilled, knowledgeable and cultured artist, influenced by Giotto's early Assisi manner and by Sienese painting. Ca. 1290-1295.

14a. *The Flood and the Return of the Dove* (south segment). The dove dispatched by Noah to look for land returns to the Ark with

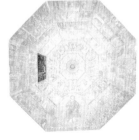

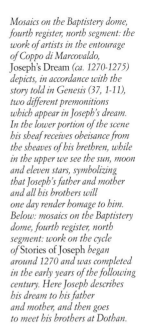

Mosaics on the Baptistery dome, fourth register, north segment: the work of artists in the entourage of Coppo di Marcovaldo, Joseph's Dream *(ca. 1270-1275)* depicts, in accordance with the story told in Genesis (37, 1-11), two different premonitions which appear in Joseph's dream. In the lower portion of the scene his sheaf receives obeisance from the sheaves of his brethren, while in the upper we see the sun, moon and eleven stars, symbolizing that Joseph's father and mother and all his brothers will one day render homage to him. Below: mosaics on the Baptistery dome, fourth register, north segment: work on the cycle of Stories of Joseph *began around 1270 and was completed in the early years of the following century. Here Joseph describes his dream to his father and mother, and then goes to meet his brothers at Dothan.*

an olive branch in its beak, a sign that the flood waters are receding. This scene was only marginally altered by the 1898-1908 restoration, but may have been retouched in earlier centuries, judging by the messy arrangement of tesserae to form the heads of the female figures. By the same artist of the Sienese school who did the preceding scene. Ca.1290-1295.

Stories of Joseph the Hebrew

In the fourth register from the top, spanning five segments, are the stories of Joseph, a Biblical figure who foreshadows the coming of Christ.

1b. *Joseph's Dream* (north segment). The sleeping Joseph dreams that the sheaves of corn bound by his brothers bow before his own, while in the sky the sun, moon, and eleven stars pay homage to him. While the three upper scenes of this segment have suffered a good deal over the ages (presumably from infiltration of rainwater) this mosaic is in fairly good shape, and can be attributed with a degree of certainty to the artist in Coppo di Marcovaldo's entourage. This and a painted cross in the Cathedral of Pistoia were probably done in the same year (1274).

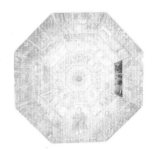

2b. *Joseph Narrates His Dream to His Father and Mother* (north segment). Under his brothers' gaze, the young Joseph narrates his dream to Jacob and Rachel. The 1898-1908 restoration somewhat altered this scene, in particular the figure of Joseph. Curiously enough, this second story of Joseph, as well as the third one, do not belong stylistically and chronologically to the present segment (whose execution in time – going from the upper to the lower levels – comes immediately after the neighbouring *Last Judgement*), but are akin to the last segment of mosaic decoration, which had already been finished in the early 14th century. In particular, we detect similarities between this and the lower register, which depicts stories of St John the Baptist. It is impossible to establish why the two stories of Joseph were included in a segment that had been completed several decades earlier, but we can tentatively suppose that the pre-existing mosaics had been damaged, or that maybe a change in the iconographic scheme was decided.

3b. *Joseph Goes to Meet his Brothers in Dothan* (north segment). Enjoined by his father, Joseph goes to meet his brothers who have taken the family sheep to graze. Here they hatch a plot to kill him. This mosaic, also somewhat altered, is the work of the late author of the preceding scene, stylistically akin to Deodato Orlandi, a painter and mosaicist who was a native of Lucca. Probably done in the early 1300s, when the mosaic program in the Baptistery was nearing completion.

4b. *Joseph is Sold by his Brothers* (north-east segment). Pulling him out of the well into which they had thrown him, Joseph's brothers sell him to a caravan of merchants. One of the best preserved mosaics in the Baptistery, despite minor 20th-century alterations in the central area and some earlier intervention. Most scholars agree that its style is strongly influenced by Cimabue, particularly in the rendition of Joseph's brothers, who closely resemble the figures of a great altarpiece depicting the *Madonna Enthroned with Angels*, now at the Louvre. Ca. 1280-1285.

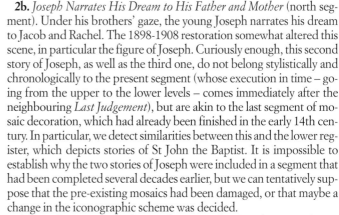

5b. *The False News of Joseph's Death* (north-east segment). Jacob and Rachel are shown the bloodied garments of Joseph, dipped by his brothers in the blood of a kid, to make them believe that Joseph was killed by a wild beast. Partly retouched, this mosaic also bears the strong imprint of Cimabue's style. This has led some authorities to attribute it to Cimabue himself, but more probably it comes from the workshop of the Master of Mary Magdalen, which in the 1280s produced a mellower and more popular version of this master's style.

6b. *Joseph is Taken to Egypt* (north-east segment). The merchants who have bought Joseph from his brothers take him to Egypt to sell him into slavery. The original parts of this mosaic include the figure of Joseph and two figures following him. As far as we can judge, this scene appears to belong to the author of the preceding one.

7b. *Joseph is Sold to Potiphar* (east segment). The merchants show Joseph to Potiphar, an official of Pharaoh, who is urged by his wife to buy him. The author of the two preceding scenes is active in this segment as well, and proves himself to be an elegant narrator, carefully inserting imaginative and lifelike details, such as the aedicule's graceful architecture and Potiphar's exotic headgear.

8b. *Potiphar's Wife Accuses Joseph* (east segment). Joseph is led off to prison after being unjustly accused by Potiphar's wife of attempting to seduce her. The subdued but eloquent pantomime, which brings into one effective sequence the woman's denunciation and Joseph's incarceration, confirms the narrative talents of this member of the Master of Mary Magdalen's workshop.

9b. *Joseph Interprets his Fellow Prisoners' Dreams* (east segment). Two episodes have been fitted into this scene. In the upper half, Pharaoh's cup-bearer and his baker, fellow prisoners of Joseph, are asleep. The former sees three fruited vines and a cup full to the brim with grapes; the latter sees a bird pecking three baskets full of bread. In the lower half of the scene, Joseph explains the meaning of these dreams: the cup-bearer will be reinstated in his job, while the baker will be hanged. The lively and fanciful narrator of these scenes achieves one of his best results in the dream scene, which strikes us with the Gothic naturalness of the sleepers' lying bodies and relaxed faces.

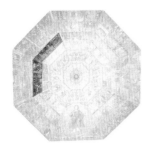

Right, mosaics on the Baptistery dome, fourth register, south-east segment: attributed to the Master of Mary Magdalen, Pharaoh's Dream *depicts the images which Joseph interprets as a prophesy of the famine that will strike Egypt. Below, mosaics on the Baptistery dome, fourth register, south-east and south segments: the* Stories of Joseph *end with his services to Pharaoh, and his reconciliation with his family.*

10b. *Pharaoh's Dream* (south-east segment). Pharaoh is asleep in his palace and dreams that seven fat cows are devoured by seven lean cows, and seven full ears of corn are swallowed by seven barren ones. In this scene only the drapery of the alcove has been restored. By the same author of the preceding episodes. His style is cultured and elegant, especially in outlining the strongly classicizing figure of the sleeping Pharaoh.

11b. *Joseph Interprets Pharaoh's Dream* (south-east segment). In the presence of Pharaoh and his ministers, Joseph declares the dream to be a divine prophecy that seven years of plenty shall be followed by seven years of famine. Here, too, this artist akin to the Master of Mary Magdalen makes use of ornamental motifs, like the winged genie on the tym-

panum of the aedicule, derived from the classical tradition, and mingles them with magical details, such as the shoots sprouting out of the architecture, reminiscent of initial letters in an illuminated manuscript.

12b. *Joseph Appointed Viceroy of Egypt* (south-east segment). Impressed by the dream which forebodes famine for Egypt and by Joseph's wise advice on how to deal with it, Pharaoh appoints Joseph Viceroy of Egypt. This is the last segment – and last scene as well – done by members of the Master of Mary Magdalen's workshop, which can be credited with a total of twenty-three scenes on the Baptistery dome. In the lower register, an anonymous artist begins the *Stories of Christ*; some scholars believe these to be the work of Giotto's friend, Gaddo Gaddi.

13b. *Laying in the Stores of Grain* (south segment). During the time of plenty, Joseph gives orders for the harvested corn to be laid up. This mosaic, whose left border was restored in 1906, is the work of the same anonymous artist who did the upper register, which includes scenes from the *Flood*. Probably trained in Siena, he worked on the mosaics on the Baptistery dome sometime between 1290 and 1295.

14b. *Joseph is Worshipped by his Brothers* (south segment). Joseph reveals his identity to his brothers, who have come to Egypt to buy grain, and makes peace with them. Similar in composition and style to the preceding scene, this mosaic can also be attributed to an artist with Sienese training, who may have worked on the frescoes in the Cathedral of Assisi, or was in any case familiar with the pictorial innovations produced by that workshop.

15b. *Joseph Meets Jacob* (south segment). Joseph sees his father again, who has come with all his family to Egypt to be reunited with him. The Sienese-like author of this scene and the preceding ones here displays a clearly Giottesque manner. This fact has prompted some authorities to attribute the scene to Giotto himself, or to sup-

Mosaics on the Baptistery dome, fourth register, south segment: Joseph Meets Jacob *was done after 1290 by an artist trained in the Sienese style. Most scholars find his manner to be extremely close to Giotto's. This is evident from a comparison between the equestrian group in this scene and the horse in the* Vision of the Fire Chariot, *one of the frescoes in the Cathedral of Assisi.*

pose that the master did the cartoons for it. There is no doubt that the author of this episode was well acquainted with the frescoes that had just been completed in Assisi. The monumental equestrian group overshadowing the whole scene does indeed remind us strongly of the similar group in the fresco *Vision of the Fire Chariot*, which Giotto did for the Assisi cycle (see p. 85).

Stories of Jesus Christ

These are in the fifth register from the top, and start – like all the story cycles on the Baptistery dome – from the north segment.

1c. *Annunciation* (north segment). According to a well-established iconographic tradition, the *Annunciation* is the first episode in the life of Jesus. The Archangel Gabriel announces to Mary that she will give birth to the Saviour, while the dove symbolizing the Holy Spirit is seen descending towards her. In earlier times this mosaic was heavily retouched, especially the face of the Madonna, and the upper half of the angel's body. Although the anonymous author of this and the two following scenes was active in the Baptistery between 1275 and 1280, he does not seem to be influenced by Cimabue's innovative style.

2c. *Visitation* (north segment). In the presence of two women, Mary goes to meet Elizabeth in front of her home. The 1906 restoration by Opificio delle Pietre Dure of this scene involved not only renovation of the bust and head of the servant girl on the left of Mary, but also of most of the central figures. The scene's composition and the architectural details suggest that its author was still inspired by Byzantine models.

3c. *Nativity* (north segment). Three angels are seen adoring the infant Christ, while a fourth brings the glad tidings to the shepherds. Joseph sits in one corner, lost in thought. Only the head and the right shoulder of the latter figure are original. The rest was thoroughly restored in 1906. Earlier alterations probably involve the heads of the Madonna and the three angels beside her. The relatively intact angel that brings

the tidings is an example of the forceful and structured manner with which this Byzantine-like author interprets Eastern models.

4c. *Adoration of the Magi* (north-east segment). The Magi have come from the East, led by the comet, and offer their gifts to the infant Jesus, on his mother's lap. In fairly good condition, this mosaic can be attributed to the workshop of the Master of Mary Magdalen. This is suggested by a similar scene on one of this prolific artist's panels now at the Musée des Arts Décoratifs, Paris.

5c. *The Dream of the Magi* (north-east segment). The Magi are told in a dream not to disclose to King Herod that they have found the Messiah. Like the preceding scene, this one too can be attributed to the workshop of the Master of Mary Magdalen. The style shows Gothic influences, especially in the dynamic pose of the sleeping Magi, and in the drapery enveloping them.

6c. *The Magi Return Home* (north-east segment). The Magi return to their lands by sea, on a sailing vessel manned by a helms-

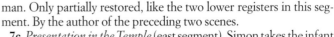

Mosaics on the Baptistery dome, fifth register, south and south-east segments: the Stories of Christ *continue with the Childhood of Jesus and the Passion. Opposite page, on the left: above,* The Flight Into Egypt, *by an artist in the entourage of the Master of the Mary Magdalen; below,* The Slaughter of the Innocents, *attributed to an artist trained in the Assisi Cathedral workshop; to the same artist is also due* The Last Supper *(on the right, above, a detail showing Christ with John, his favourite disciple); below, detail of the* Coronation of the Virgin, *a mosaic which decorates a lunette in Florence Cathedral: its stylistic features do indeed remind us of the mosaics of the* Stories of Christ *attributed to this artist.*

man. Only partially restored, like the two lower registers in this segment. By the author of the preceding two scenes.

7c. *Presentation in the Temple* (east segment). Simon takes the infant Jesus from the hands of the Virgin Mary and Joseph (who brings two doves as gifts to the Temple) and raises him up. The aged prophetess Ann witnesses the scene. Heavy restoration has altered Simon, and in part also the other figures. Nonetheless, the analogies between this scene and the stories on the above-mentioned panel painting by the Master of Mary Magdalen are quite evident.

8c. *St Joseph's Dream* (east segment). An angel appears to Joseph in dream and urges him to flee from King Herod with his wife and child. FUGE IN EGIPTUM, "Flee into Egypt", are the words we read on the scroll the angel holds in his hands. The 1906 restoration is so thorough that a reading of the original style is well nigh impossible. However, given its position in this series of scenes, we can suppose it to belong to the workshop of the Master of Mary Magdalen.

9c. *Flight into Egypt* (east segment). The Virgin Mary and the infant Jesus are seated on a mount, preceded by a servant and followed by St Joseph. Only very lightly retouched, this scene is akin to the *Flight into Egypt* in the abovementioned painting by the Master of Mary Magdalen (see 4c). It, too, has in common with it a number of details, like the stylized crowns of the trees, which remind us once again of the techniques used in manuscript illumination.

10c. *Slaughter of the Innocents* (south-east segment). Seated upon a throne in the form of a niche, Herod watches the slaughter of all male children, which is carried out amidst the desperation of the mothers. This is the first scene executed by a new and brilliant artist who worked on the mosaics of the Baptistery dome between 1290 and 1295. Earlier authorities identified him with Gaddo Gaddi. The Cimabue-like character and the monumental scale of this scene remind us of painting in Rome in the same period. The author probably imbibed these influences from the Assisi frescoes, which in the last quarter of the

1200s brought together all the latest trends in European painting.

11c. *The Last Supper* (south-east segment). Christ is seated at a round table together with the Apostles. We see the kneeling Judas in the foreground. Much altered by restoration. The only authentic zones appear to be the kneeling Judas and Christ. The latter resembles the Christ in the *Coronation of the Virgin Mary*, situated on the counter-façade of Santa Maria del Fiore, and probably authored by the same artist a few years earlier.

12c. *Capture of Christ* (south-east segment). Mingling with the crowd that has come to capture Christ, Judas approaches him to betray him with a kiss, while Peter pulls out a knife and smites the ear of Malchus, a servant of the High Priest. The area on the right – including the fig-

Mosaics on the Baptistery dome, fifth register, south-east segment: Capture of Christ, *detail. This scene was done around 1290 by the artist trained in Assisi mentioned above; not coincidentally there is a remarkable stylistic correlation between this work and the same subject painted in the Basilica of Assisi (see below). Bottom of page: mosaics on the Baptistery dome, fifth register, south segment. The* Stories of Christ *end with the Crucifixion, the Lamentation (both attributed to Lippo di Benivieni) and the Women at the Holy Sepulchre.*

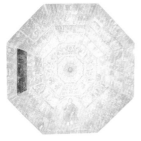

ure of Christ – appears to be the least retouched of this scene. The author's stay in Assisi is suggested by the similarity in style and composition between this mosaic and the fresco depicting the *Capture of Christ* in the basilica of Assisi.

13c. *Crucifixion* (south segment). To the left of Christ Crucified we see the Madonna, who has fainted and is assisted by the pious women. On the right hand side is St John the Evangelist, together with a third female figure. We know that in 1489 the painter Alessio Baldovinetti, who spent a long period restoring the mosaics in the Baptistery, filled in a gap here. The Christ Crucified in this scene is one of the oldest such figures directly inspired by the innovative *Crucifix* which Giotto painted in the late 13th century in Santa Maria Novella. This scene and the neighbouring *Lamentation* (both of which can be dated around 1300) are the only two mosaics done by this artist in the Baptistery. In them we detect the new Giottesque features, still somewhat held back by typical 13th-century training. The author could be Lippo di Bienivieni, who in 1313-1315 painted a tabernacle for the Baptistery (no longer extant).

14c. *Lamenting the Death of Christ* (south segment). This scene takes place at the foot of the Cross. Mary Magdalen raises her arms in a ges-

Mosaics on the Baptistery dome, fifth register, south segment: The Lamentation is attributed to Lippo di Benivieni and was probably done in the early years of the 14th century.
Below, mosaics on the Baptistery dome, sixth register, north segment: the Stories of St John the Baptist – which at that time had a precedent in similar cycles in the Baptisteries of Pisa and Parma – begin with the appearance of the Archangel Gabriel before Zechariah. The scenes of this Announcement and the Birth of St John are followed by the story of his ascetic retreat into the wilderness.

ture of grief, while the Madonna and St John hold up the body of Christ. To the right of the two women are Nicodemus and Joseph of Arimathea. The evident similarities between this mosaic and a painting attributed to Lippo di Bienivieni (now in the Museo Civico of Pistoia), lead us to conjecture that this artist did both works. Lippo reached artistic maturity at a time when painting was still under the influence of Cimabue: nevertheless, he readily welcomed the innovations arising out of Giotto's work.

15c. *The Women at the Sepulchre* (south segment). The pious women come to the tomb of Christ, and find the guards fast asleep. Just then an angel appears to proclaim the Resurrection of Christ. Somewhat altered, especially the heads of the women and the angel, this mosaic appears to be the work of an artist of Sienese and Assisi extraction, who also did the scenes in the two upper registers of this segment.

Stories of St John the Baptist

In the sixth and last register from the top, spanning five segments, are fifteen stories of St John the Baptist, the city's patron Saint, to whom the Baptistery is dedicated.

Mosaics on the Baptistery dome, sixth register, north segment: the scene narrating The Birth of St John and His Naming *(detail shown on the right) was done between 1280 and 1285 by an artist stylistically related to Cimabue. Opposite page, above,* The Youthful St John Withdraws into the Wilderness, *by the same artist. In the scroll we read the words with which, according to the Scriptures, St John the Baptist addressed the multitudes exhorting them to repent for their sins. Opposite page, below, mosaics on the Baptistery dome, sixth register, north-east segment:* The Stories of St John the Baptist *continue with a scene narrating how the Saint preaches to the multitudes and baptizes them, while announcing the coming of the Messiah.*

1d. *Announcement to Zechariah* (north segment). In the garb of a priest, Zechariah offers incense in the Temple crowded by the faithful. The Archangel Gabriel appears to announce to him that a son named John will be born to him. The 1906 restoration has strongly retouched the right-hand portion of this scene, while the figures of Zechariah and the Angel must have undergone overhauling in an earlier period. The mosaic's general design seems to be based on a cartoon that is similar to the preliminary drawing for the *Annunciation* scene directly overhead, authored by a Florentine artist not yet influenced by Cimabue. This is the only scene of the cycle of St John the Baptist that can be attributed to him.

2d. *Birth and Naming of St John the Baptist* (north segment). The scene combines two events. On the left, is the birth of the Baptist; on the right, Zechariah, whom the Lord has struck dumb for his reluctance to believe the news of the late birth of a son, is writing on a tablet the appointed name of the new-born child. Due to repeated restoration, the original features of this mosaic can be detected only in the figure of Zechariah and in the head of his young attendant (the last figure on the right of the central group). Some authorities have singled out this head for the high quality of its design and execution, going as far as to attribute it to Cimabue himself. Indeed, while the figure of Zechariah and other areas of the mosaic may be ascribed to the follower of Cimabue who did the upper registers of the next segment, the head of the young attendant in this scene shows a more refined handling and may have been added by a more talented artist.

3d. *The Youthful John in the Wilderness* (north segment). The youthful John in the desert waits until the time is ripe for him to preach. In his hand he holds a scroll with the scriptural injunction: "Do ye works of penance". A marble plate inserted at the foot of the rocks marks the 1907 restoration: "from 1898 to 1907 the Royal Opificio delle Pietre Dure, under the supervision of Florence Cathedral's Opera and with the assistance of its workmen, reinforced, restored, and reset the mosaics in this dome, which through long neglect had been dimmed and were in a state of disrepair". The restoration overhauled most of this scene and caused alterations which do not allow us to make any exact statements about it. Physically and stylistically it would seem to belong to the group of scenes most strongly influenced by Cimabue.

4d. *St John the Baptist Preaches to the Crowds* (north-east segment). St John preaches to the people, holding in his left hand a scroll which reads VOX CLAMANTIS IN DESERTO, "a voice crying in the wilderness". In spite of some slight stylistic differences (probably due to different craftsmen working on the same cartoons), the three stories of St John

Mosaics on the Baptistery dome, sixth register, east segment: after the Baptism of Christ, the stories of this cycle depict the conflict between St John the Baptist and Herod, Tetrarch of Galilee, who subsequently has St John cast into prison.

the Baptist included in this section seem to belong to the member of the workshop of the Master of Mary Magdalen who did the upper register, as well as the three stories of Christ in the following segment.

5d. *Baptism of the Crowds* (north-east segment). St John baptizes a disciple with water from the River Jordan, while a group of his followers witness the event. By the artist associated with the Master of Mary Magdalen, and author of most of the stories on the Baptistery dome.

6d. *St John Announces the Coming of Christ* (north-east segment). At the centre of this scene, St John the Baptist points Christ out to the crowd, just as Christ is seen coming out from behind a rock, his hand raised in blessing. In his left hand, St John holds a scroll which reads: ECCE AGNUS DEI ECCE QUI TOLLIT, "Behold the Lamb of God, behold Him Who Removes (the Sins of the World)". The scene's authorship is the same as the preceding ones.

7d. *Baptism of Christ* (east segment). Two angels bringing garments witness the baptism of Christ in the waters of the River Jordan. Several stylistic influences mingle in all the scenes created by the Master of Mary Magdalen's workshop: the three stories of St John the Baptist in this segment are the ones most clearly influenced by contemporary Byzantine art.

8d. *St John the Baptist Reproaches Herod* (east segment). Followed by two disciples, St John appears before King Herod to reproach him for having taken for wife Herodias, who was already married to the Tetrarch's brother. Herod's head and the left-hand portion of his body were redone during the 1907 restoration. This scene, like the preceding ones, can also be attributed to the Master of Mary Magdalen's workshop. Here, as in the stories of *Joseph the Hebrew* in the neighbouring segment, the narration is enriched with classicizing ornament, such as the servant girl with the *flabellum*, or the Roman-style architecture of the arch.

9d. *St John the Baptist is Thrown into Prison* (east segment). Herodias orders the Tetrarch's soldiers to capture St John. In fairly good condition, this scene is by the same anonymous artist in the entourage of the Master of Mary Magdalen, and displays his talent for cultured and imaginative decorative detail – like the small trees that grow out of the classical tympanum of the prison, or the guard's elaborate armour and crested helmet.

10d. *St John the Baptist sends His Disciples to Christ* (south-east segment). While languishing in prison, St John is apprised of the work of Jesus, and sends two disciples to ask him if he is the expected Messiah. This mosaic is part of the six successive scenes (in the next-to-last and last registers of the fourth segment) authored by the great artist

Below, mosaics on the Baptistery dome, sixth register, south-east and south segments: by the same Assisi-trained artist mentioned above, who worked in Florence's Baptistery in the final years of the 13th century. The three scenes from the Stories of St John *narrated in the south-east segment include* St John sending two of his disciples to meet the Saviour, St John's Disciples Witness Christ's Miracles *(detail shown on the left) and a scene in which* Salome dances for St John's head. *We come now to the scenes in the south segment, attributed to the Lucca artist Deodato Orlandi: the cycle ends with* St John's beheading and his burial.

who was influenced by the Assisi frescoes. Here this anonymous master confirms his artistic proximity to the Master of *The Capture of Christ*. The forceful handling of the two apostles taking leave of St John the Baptist reminds us closely of the Roman soldier walking ahead of Christ in the *Road to Calvary* in Assisi.

11d. *Christ Performs Miracles in Front of St John the Baptist's Disciples* (south-east segment). In the presence of the Baptist's envoys, Christ performs a number of awe-inspiring miracles. This mosaic is riddled with old refurbishing which has also altered the disciples, although these are in somewhat better condition. All we can do, then, is attribute this scene to the group of six impressive and troubled scenes done by the artist who worked on the Assisi frescoes.

12d. *Salome's Dance* (south-east segment). Herodias' daughter Salome dances in honour of King Herod, who is at a banquet with his wife and some guests. With the possible exception of Salome, all the other figures were restored in earlier centuries. The monumental scale

Mosaics on the Baptistery dome, sixth register, south segment: the scene in which Salome brings St John the Baptist's head to Herodias *(detail shown here) has been attributed to Deodato Orlandi. Executed in the early years of the 13th century.*

of the composition and the dynamic body language of the figures are recognizable as the work of the author of the preceding scenes. It is possible that his cartoons, done about 1290-1295, were turned into mosaics some time later. Salome's dress suggests this, for it is modelled on women's fashions of the early 1300s.

13d. *Beheading of St John the Baptist* (south segment). Salome brings Herod's order for the beheading of St John the Baptist, and watches the execution in the jail. The 1898-1908 restoration reset the executioner's garments and filled in a number of minor blank spaces. The author of this last register on the Baptistery dome – who probably also did the second and third stories of Joseph in the first segment of the dome – may have been one of a group of early-14th-century artists who used Giotto's language to develop a somewhat insipid and conversational style of his own. In Florence, one of the most prolific representatives of this trend was the painter and miniature artist Pacino di Buonaguida: these last mosaics have several points in common with his style, but they are even more reminiscent of another popularizer of Giotto's innovations, the Lucca painter and mosaicist Deodato Orlandi.

14d. *Salome Takes St John the Baptist's Head to Herodias* (south segment). Accompanied by the executioner, Salome offers St John the Baptist's head to Herodias, who is feasting with King Herod. The kneeling figure on the right-hand side of the scene has been heavily altered by an early restoration. By an artist influenced by Giotto, maybe Deodato Orlandi. In the left-hand section of the aedicule the dentils were seen as if from the front and then corrected in perspective: this was certainly made at the time that the mosaic was being set, and suggests that its author's 13th-century training had not yet enabled him to fully master Giotto's more rational handling of space.

15d *Burial of St John the Baptist* (south segment). St John's disciples lower his body into a sarcophagus. The affinity between this scene and Deodato Orlandi's fresco the *Burial of St Peter* in the church of San Piero a Grado, near Pisa, seem to confirm that these last stories, probably dating from the early years of the 14th century, are his work.

The Mosaics in the Apse

The *scarsella*, though restricted in size, is also resplendent with a spread of mosaics covering both the triumphal arch and its flat barrel vaulted ceiling.

A double decorative band spans the front of the arch. The external band is traversed by a fruited vine climbing up from two symbolic nude figures leaning on wild beasts. In the central medallion is a bust of *Christ Raising His Hand in Blessing*. On the other band, inside panels framed by decorative strips, is a series of sixteen busts of *Apostles*, *Evangelists* and *Saints*, each of which is identified by an inscription. *St John the Baptist* is depicted at the centre of the row of busts, directly above the altar dedicated to him.

On the interior curve, or intrados, of the round arch we see a series of superimposed aedicules, containing the full-length figures of twelve

The triumphal arch at the entrance of the "scarsella" is decorated with a double band of mosaics. At the centre of the outer band is Christ Raising His Hand in Blessing, *while the inner one consists of a series of busts of Apostles, Evangelists and Saints depicted in the Byzantine style. On the arch's intrados are twelve Prophets. With the exception of the figure of* Hosea *(below, to the left of* Habakkuk *and* Haggai*), all these have been heavily restored.*

At the summit of the apse's domical, or cloister, vault is a wheel held up by four Atlas figures kneeling on Corinthian capitals. Inside the wheel is a representation of the Mystic Lamb, between candelabra and Prophets (see detail below). At the sides are four corner tablets containing a disputed inscription, which states that the mosaic decoration in this zone was begun 12 May, 1225 – the ninth year of the rule of Pope Onophrius III (1216-1227), and the fifth in the reign of Frederic II of Swabia (1220-1250) – by a Franciscan friar by the name of Jacopo. Vasari identifies this figure with Jacopo da Torrita, who authored the frescoes in San Giovanni in Laterano and Santa Maria Maggiore in Rome. The inscription's authenticity, however, is dubious, since the stylistic characters of these mosaics have no parallel in Florentine painting until 1260. Opposite page, below, the Madonna enthroned with Child portrayed on the right hand side of the vault. This mosaic was almost entirely redone in 1908. Right, the four Atlas figures holding up the central wheel.

Prophets, identified by Latin inscriptions. At the centre is a bust of the Virgin Mary. In the past, this area must have experienced serious conservation problems, as the figures of the prophets appear to have been heavily restored. In some cases, intervention went so far as to alter the repetitive model of the aedicule. The only figure that conserves its original appearance is the Prophet *Hosea* (in the first aedicule at the bottom left hand corner), which can be attributed to an artist working in the Florentine-Pisan style sometime between 1256 and 1275.

The damage (probably due to rainwater leaking in) as well as the subsequent alterations appear to be sweeping here, particularly on the apse's ceiling. At the ceiling's summit, there is a large wheel with a medallion at its centre containing the *Mystical Lamb*. The medallion is bordered by a red band with a Latin inscription in gold tesserae which reads: "Behold the Almighty God indicated by the meek Lamb". The inside of the wheel is divided into sections by eight candelabra-shaped 'spokes', alternated by eight full-length figures of Biblical *Patriarchs* and *Prophets*.

In the corner pendentives of the vaulted ceiling, the wheel described above is held up by four massive Atlas figures kneeling on Corinthian capitals. Beneath these figures are four tablets with a red background containing a Latin verse inscription in gold lettering, whose meaning is disputed (see below). At the sides of the ceiling, in the area marked off by the corner Atlas figures, we see a *Madonna Enthroned with Child* on the right, and *St John the Baptist Enthroned* on the left. Here heavy renovation also affected the figures in the central wheel and the telamons themselves, thus strongly altering their original appearance. The image of the *Madonna* is largely the fruit of Opificio's 1898-1908 restoration in 'Medieval' style. At that time the original mosaic no longer existed, having been replaced by a mural painting, probably in the 18th century. The painting can be seen in photographs of the *scarsella* taken before 1908.

Even though over-restoring and alterations have made it difficult to appreciate the mosaics' original style, their date of execution has nev-

er been seriously challenged. The inscription spanning the four corner tablets testifies that "this work" (*hoc opus*) was completed on 12 May 1225, by Jacopo, a Franciscan friar and expert mosaicist. Yet its text is perplexingly ambiguous. Firstly, it designates Francis of Assisi as a Saint three years before he was actually sainted (1228). In the second place, the style of the Fra' Jacopo who is supposed to have authored these mosaics (maybe Jacopo Torriti, a native of Rome who was active around the end of the 13th century), is not recognizable in the mosaics of the *scarsella*, nor in those of the Baptistery dome. Finally, the inscription mentions Emperor Frederick II of Swabia, with whom Florence's relations in 1225 were strained, to say the least. It is a fair guess that the inscription is more recent, which would also explain the incorrect information it contains. Moreover, a cautious stylistic study of the mosaics in the *scarsella* suggests they are less in harmony with the artistic canons current in the first half of the 13th century, than with those that emerged between 1260 and 1270. The forceful Atlas figures remind us of the painting of the Florentine Coppo di Marcovaldo – at the time still influenced by Giunta Pisano – while the well preserved busts of saints on the arch's decorative band are notable for their graceful Byzantine lines and can thus be directly linked to the Pisan culture that produced the Master of St Martin.

The foregoing would seem to indicate that the mosaics of the dome were not, as often claimed, accomplished by the artists of the *scarsella*. The *scarsella* entered the picture only when the colossal job on the dome was already well under way and sufficiently tested, so to speak. Thus the exact opposite is probably closer to the mark – i.e., the swift progress in mosaicking the dome prompted the Baptistery's patrons to extend their decorative project to the *scarsella* and to other parts of the building.

The Mosaics on the Drum of the Dome

While the decoration of the Baptistery dome and *scarsella* was nearing completion, work began on the great drum-shaped base of the dome and on the women's gallery.

The eight sides of the drum are covered with twenty-six mosaic panels. More or less square in shape, these panels portray the busts of seven *Popes*, *Bishops* and *Deacons* who achieved sainthood. Probably created in the first decade of the 14th century, they were set on top of pre-existing marble inlays. Indeed, recent restoration work of two sides of the drum has uncovered slabs of serpentine marble from Prato hidden beneath the mosaics. Their surface was previously pockmarked with a chisel to enable the mortar bed (underlying the tesserae) to adhere better. This suggests that originally there was no project to mosaic this area, and that such work was undertaken only when the imposing mosaics on the dome proved themselves to be a more eloquent illustration of the fundamental truths of the Christian creed than the abstract marble inlays.

Starting from the eastern side of the drum – facing the Cathedral – and proceeding in clockwise motion, are the busts of the following saints (each identified by a Latin inscription): *Bishop Basil, Bishop*

John, Deacon Parmenas, Bishop Dennis, Bishop Ignatius, Deacon Nikanor, Bishop Nicholas, Pope Sylvester, Philip the Deacon, Bishop Isidore, Pope Leo the Great, Stephen the Deacon, Bishop Augustine, Bishop Jerome, Pope Gregory, Bishop Ambrose, Lawrence the Deacon, Bishop Zenobius, Bishop Hilarion, V[...] the Deacon, Bishop Martin, Bishop Fulgentius, V[incent?] the Deacon, Bishop Cyprian, Bishop Gregory and *Prochorius the Deacon.*

The same two masters who completed the mosaics in the women's gallery did part of the mosaics on the drum. Albeit trained in the 13th century, both these artists were already under the sway of Giotto's new pictorial language. The artist with the more old-fashioned style may well be the Master of San Gaggio. At first similar to the Master of Mary Magdalen, he underwent a degree of 'modernization' in Giottesque terms, without however relinquishing certain forms and expressions typical of 13th-century painting before Giotto. On the base of the dome his contribution, achieved in partnership with the second artist, seems to be restricted to the side above the *scarsella* – the only one that has four mosaic panels – and to the south-west and south sides next to it. His strongly 13th-century style is especially clear in the detail of *St Augustine* above the *scarsella*, and in the *St Nicholas* on the south side. Both figures are somewhat stiff, lacking in depth and marked by strong areas of shade.

Here, as well as in the inner rooms of the women's gallery, the second artist is stylistically so consecutive to the first that we may suppose that he was trained in the former's workshop. Yet he is distinguished for a more Giottesque style. Amongst the Florentine artists of the 14th century who profited from this master's tactile and chiaroscuro innova-

Above, mosaics on the panels covering the dome's drum. The following saints are depicted here: John *(east),* Ignatius *(south-east),* Zenobius *(west),* Ambrose, Hilarion *(north-west),* and Fulgentius *(north). With the exception of the figure of* St Ambrose, *attributed to the Master of San Gaggio, these portraits are thought to be by the Master of St Cecily.*

tions, it is the anonymous Master of Saint Cecily who strikes us as being closest to the mosaics in the Baptistery. Indeed, he can be credited with authorship of the cartoons. His hand can be recognized in a number of busts on the abovementioned walls because of the Gothic touch in the outlines and drapery, as well as in the soft shading of the faces. *St Sylvester* on the south side and *St Gregory* above the *scarsella* are examples of this. Furthermore, he was personally responsible for the preliminary drawings for the busts covering the remaining five sides of the drum, for they are shown strictly from the front, like Giotto's early work in Assisi (notably in the decoration of the arches in the Vault of the Doctors). This artist's incomplete mastery of Giotto's spatial dynamics can be discerned also in his perspectival difficulty in making the patterns on the garments agree with the folds. It is no coincidence that this problem was left unsolved by the Master of St Cecily as well. Another telltale detail that links the mosaics of the Baptistery to the works of this anonymous Giottesque artist is the archaic rendering of the figures' ears, seen from the front.

Some authorities have suggested that the Master of St Cecily was none other than the Gaddo Gaddi mentioned by Vasari as Giotto's friend and follower. This theory could be supported by the stylistic affinities between the artist who did the latest mosaics in the Baptistery and the Master of St Cecily.

The uneven quality of the busts decorating the drum depend on the fact that, around 1310, different artists set these mosaics which were modelled on cartoons prepared by two artists only. Situated in one of the most protected areas inside the Baptistery, they are amongst the best-preserved parts of the entire mosaic cycle, so much so that it is hard to detect signs of restoration on them. Nevertheless, we know from documents that in 1488 Baldovinetti carried out one minor restoration (perhaps on the figures of *St Leo* and *St Isidore* on the wall to the left of the *scarsella*), as they required "mending".

The Mosaics in the Women's Gallery

Decoration of the Gallery Sections

In the early 14th century the project to extend the mosaics to areas of the Baptistery beyond the dome eventually came to include also part of the women's gallery, which – as we saw above – was at that time decorated with bichrome mural paintings.

Mosaics decorate three adjacent sections of the gallery above the east portal, or Gates of Paradise, and one section above the south doors. This suggests that the original project provided for decoration of one section above each of the side entrances, and three sections above the main one. The job was left unfinished, since the section above the north doors has no wall painting, suggesting that the plaster was removed to prepare the wall for the mosaics. The coretti are only partially visible from the ground floor, and the viewer perceives them just as luminous and indefinite amplifications of the gallery. Probably because of their more protected location, the mosaics here were not included in Opificio's 1898-1908-restoration program. The older integrations, painted in tempera on the plaster in a quick and lively manner, were probably executed during the renovation of 1782. Later integrations were done more delicately, by painting a checquered colour pattern on the plaster, in imitation of mosaic tesserae. Other more recent and coarser intervention was done with concrete mortar. At present, Opificio delle Pietre Dure and Opera del Duomo are collaborating on a scheme to refurbish and reinforce the gallery sections above the east portal, and fill the gaps in the mosaics there.

The mosaics in the gallery appear to have been completed rather rapidly. The work in and outside this area may have started from the section over the south portal, because the author of these mosaics – the Master of San Gaggio – probably also did the stylistically more archaic busts of the *Prophets* on the first two parapet sections left of the *scarsella* (south-west and south walls).

The mosaics in the gallery's south section are organized like those in the other three sections. In the area, which opens on the interior of the Baptistery through a mullioned window with two lights, they start at about a metre and a half from floor level and spread across all three walls, the barrel vaulted ceiling and the lunette above the mullioned window. The compositional criteria in the four inner sections also follow a uniform scheme. On the vault and the side walls are a series of medallions containing half-length portraits. Above the mullioned window with two lights is a single, larger medallion containing a half-length figure between two grotesques. On the exterior wall, which has a window, are full-length figures of saints standing in niches. In the embrasure of the window is a circle of medallions of a pair of affronted saints. There is plenty of similar ornamental detail in all the sections: examples are the animal and human grotesques which, like those in illuminated manuscripts, blend with creepers; the medallions, formed by plant volutes or interlaced with clusters of leaves; finally, the wealth of sinuous acanthus leaves, depicted in a variety of colours and combinations.

Attributed to the circle of the Master of St Gaggio, the mosaics in the middle section at the south end of the women's gallery (also called section "of the male busts") were done between 1300 and 1310. The medallions on the vault enclose busts of hermits, laymen and monks. The meaning of these figures has yet to be fully explored.

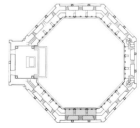

Although united by a common compositional structure, the mosaics in these four sections follow different iconographic schemes. The symbolic theme pictured in the south room remains obscure: the medallions contain busts of male figures of varying age and social condition: hermits, monks, a friar, venerable old men, a young man who grasps a rolled-up scroll, and a pair of figures engaged in conversation, wearing garments and headgear modelled on early-14th-century fashions. Above the mullioned window with two lights, inside an almond-shaped zone inside the lunette, is the central half-length figure of a young king standing between two winged genii on horseback, grasping acanthus leaves. On the wall, inside niches, are two full-length figures depicting the Apostles *Thomas* and *Andrew* as young men. These figures, sketched with a rather stiff hand and marked by sharp chiaroscuro contrasts, remind us of the Master of San Gaggio. His more up-to-date partner (the Master of St Cecily?) worked on the mosaics in the three gallery sections above the Gates of Paradise.

The first of these, bordering on the north-east wall (to the left of the viewer), depicts the *Angelic Choirs*. While in the upper register of the dome these classes of heavenly beings are identified with a caption, here no explanations or specific attributes are given to help us distinguish between them. However, the largest half-length figure above the mullioned window with two lights, standing between two nude grotesques looking out from behind acanthus leaves, probably de-

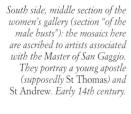

South side, middle section of the women's gallery (section "of the male busts"): the mosaics here are ascribed to artists associated with the Master of San Gaggio. They portray a young apostle (supposedly St Thomas*) and* St Andrew. *Early 14th century.*

picts the *Archangel Michael*. Many tesserae and sections of mortar in
the lower portion of this area had given way; indeed, the mosaic was
in danger of being lost entirely because the old binder was slowly de-
caying. In the 1980s, Opificio delle Pietre Dure removed the mosaics
from the wall, and reset them on a new bed that was fixed to the wall
with screws. The decoration in this section is completed by the full-
length figures of *St Philip* (on the wall beside the window), *St James
the Younger* and *St Matthew* (on the interior sides of the window). The
rough execution that sometimes characterizes these figures suggests
the authorship of the Master of San Gaggio, who worked in the same
workshop as the Master of St Cecily. The latter appears to have done
only some of the angels in the vault. Their stronger Giottesque character is noticeable in the soft shading, somewhat soft three-dimen-
sional quality of the faces and subtle chromatic variations on the figures' silky garments.

In the central section, or *"coretto* of the Evangelists", the vaulted
ceiling is decorated with a series of five multifoil decorations, now
much damaged, enclosing the *Mystic Lamb* at the centre and the symbols of the four Evangelists on either side. In the lunette above the
mullioned window with two lights – inside a medallion formed by
acanthus volutes springing out of a vase – is the half-length figure of
Christ Raising His Hand in Blessing. On either side of the window are
full-length figures of *St Peter* and *St Paul* standing inside niches. On

The saint portrayed in the third
section on the gallery's east side
– also called section "of the Holy
Virgins" – is thought to be
St Thaddeus. The decoration
of this section has been attributed
to an artist associated with
the Master of San Gaggio,
perhaps aided by the Master
of Santa Cecilia. Early
14th century, restored 1994.

Right: the 14th century mosaics on the vault in the gallery section "of the Holy Virgins" portray St Lucy and St Margaret. Below, the middle section (also called "of the Evangelists") in the eastern zone of the women's gallery. The eagle of St John and the angel symbolizing St Matthew used to flank a representation of the Mystical Lamb which has been lost.

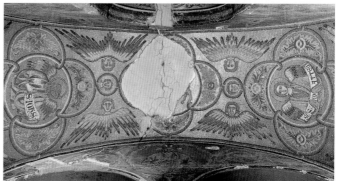

the interior sides of the window *St Zenobius* stands opposite *St Reparata* (together with St John the Baptist, the patron Saints of Florence). This area, as well as the lunette, can be credited to the Master of St Gaggio, while the Master of St Cecily did the multifoil decorations in the vault.

The third section of the gallery (to the right of the viewer) portrays the Holy Virgins. In the geometric medallions on the ceiling are busts of *St Agnes, St Margaret, St Lucy* and *St Catherine*, each identified with her attributes and an inscription. Between one medallion and the other are pairs of angels, while the vault's summit displays a star-spangled medallion. In the lunette three volutes of creepers enclose a venerable old man flanked by two male figures facing him. The scene is obscure, but might symbolize the three ages of man. On the wall with the window is a niche containing *St Thaddeus*. On the interior sides of the window *St John the Apostle* stands facing *St Simon*. Examples of a more mature Giottesque style, these two figures – together with the figures of *St Agnes* and *St Lucy* on the ceiling – can be ascribed to the Master of St Cecily, while the other portions of the mosaic are by the Master of St Gaggio. Probably in the 1700s the pair of small heads of angels below *St Catherine* were retouched with pictorial integrations, albeit tastefully. The other restoring we detect here and in other mosaics in the women's gallery is later and more roughly executed, either with a checquered pattern painted on plaster, or simply filled in with concrete mortar.

The Two Ornamental Friezes

The mosaics in the women's gallery are completed by two ornamental friezes running above and below the *loggetta*, and by the panels on the parapets.

The two friezes cover the pre-existing marble entablature, or horizontal beam. Set on terracotta slabs fixed to the marble inlays, they were made shortly after the early 14th century. Both friezes run along the gallery's outer sides, and each repeats a particular design. The upper motif consists of a series of acanthus leaves with human profiles sprouting out of them, the lower one of a succession of busts of lively *Cherubim* and *Seraphim*, winking at the viewer. The expressive features of these figures, as well as a taste for grotesque invention and vivid colouring, suggest that this mosaic is the work of the early-14th-century Florentine workshop which also did the mosaics in the gallery sections and on the architrave above the Pisano doors. The latter in fact has three medallions of acanthus leaves flanked by a pair of volutes and enclosing three small heads of angels. The central medallion is little more than a blurred mass today, having been altered by over-restoration. Nevertheless, the design of the two other angels and the coils is so similar to the angels on the frieze, that we can consider them both to belong to the same period and workshop.

The decision to extend the mosaic decoration to the portals of the building was launched in the early 1300s, but did not get further than the south doors until – 150 years later – Alessio Baldovinetti mosaicked the architraves of the other two doors.

It is possible that several artists, reproducing the same motifs in series, completed the two friezes in a relatively short space of time the two friezes that run along the outside wall of the women's gallery. Indeed, they are in fairly good condition, having been only lightly integrated with patches of painted plaster at a later date. Baldovinetti's conservation work here, mentioned in his memoirs, *Ricordi*, has not been identified. On the north-east wall, about three quarters of the frieze depicting cherubim was replaced by a panel painting which imitates its design. This probably dates from the late 16th, early 17th centuries, and was carried out in conjunction with two refurbishing schemes involving the 14th-century Crucifix altar, which up to the early 1900s stood against this same wall.

The frieze depicting Cherubim *and* Seraphim *runs along seven sides of the Baptistery building. It was done in the early 1300s by artists associated with the Master of San Gaggio. At a later time a substantial part of the mosaic decoration in this north-east area was replaced with a painted wooden panel which reproduces the original motifs.*

The Mosaics on the Parapets

The mosaics on the parapets are more impressive and artistically significant. Six busts of Prophets holding scrolls occupied each of the gallery's seven sides. Thirty-six busts have survived to the present day: the six on the east wall, above the Gates of Paradise, were torn down in 1782, when this section of the gallery was chosen to house a new organ with a projecting choir gallery.

Recent renovation of the parapets of the first two walls to the left of the *scarsella* has revealed the technique that was used to set up the panels. Since the parapet's smooth marble slabs would not have been able to support the mortar setting bed, a number of holes made from the back were fitted with iron rivets, and terracotta panels were fixed to these. Before baking, notches had been scratched into the panel surfaces to enable the mortar to adhere more easily. The mortar was spread in one go. This singular solution was made possible by the fact that the marble slabs were recessed 5 cm deeper than their frame, thus leaving a sufficient thickness for the terracotta panels, the layer of mortar and the mosaic tesserae. Before spreading the mortar, a rough sinopia was sketched on the terracotta panels. Such preliminary drawings were presumably used for all the mosaics in the Baptistery. Strong evidence of this practice was found here when two busts were removed from the south-west wall during restoration (see below).

Although the mosaics on the parapets – like those inside the women's gallery – were not touched by the restoration campaign launched in the early years of the 20th century, they had often been refurbished in earlier times, starting with Alessio Baldovinetti's 15th-century integration with mosaic pieces – his work being at times hardly discernible – right up to 18th- and 19th-century integrations with checquered patterns painted on plaster.

Six sides of the gallery's parapet are covered by mosaic decoration depicting busts of Prophets. While the mosaics on the east wall were removed in 1782 to make way for a new organ and choir, those on the south and south-west walls were recently restored. Below, the south parapet. Visitors can make out one of the four mosaicked sections of the gallery (and precisely the one known as the section "of the male busts") through the mullioned window with two lights.

Left, a detail of the figures on the parapet of the gallery's south section: Baruch, Noah, Joshua, Samuel, Elisha *and* Simon *"Oni(a)e filius". These busts were executed early in the 14th century by artists associated with the Master of San Gaggio.*

The bust of *Samuel* has incurred the worst damage. The missing head was patched up probably in the late 18th century with a coarse checquered pattern painted on plaster by two unknown painters, Orlandini and Sorbolini. During recent refurbishing work done on this parapet and that of the adjacent south-west wall, these patches (which were previously removed and rested on an underlying support to help preserve them) were replaced with mosaic tesserae that imitate the earlier refurbishing but evoke only a hazy picture of it. This solution allowed restorers to avoid falsifying the head – whose original appearance is unknown – but at the same time does not attract too much attention to the mutilation.

During the same campaign, two crumbling mosaics on the south-west wall portraying *Moses* and *Elijah* were removed, and set on a new bed of mortar directly on the wall. As we mentioned above, this intervention revealed the underlying sinopias of both these images, roughly outlined in red on the terracotta panels.

On the parapet of the wall next to the *scarsella* have thus been restored – proceeding, as usual, from right to left – the busts of *Moses, Jacob, Isaac, Abraham, Enoch, Elijah*; on the south wall are represented *Baruch, Noah, Joshua, Samuel, Elisha* and *Simon* "Oniae filius", or "son of Onias".

The mosaics on the parapets of the south-east wall (to the right of the portal facing the Cathedral) were so heavily retouched and altered in earlier times that in many cases it is no longer possible to appreciate their original features. This will be easier to do when the present renovation program – which at this point in time has not progressed beyond the two walls to the right of the *scarsella* – focusses on this area. The prophets portrayed are *Jesus son of Iosedech, Zorobabel, Ezra, Nehemiah, Judas Maccabeus* and *Mattathias*. Baldovinetti mentions the mosaics on this wall in a note of 1490, in which he discusses the refurbishing work he did "on the white and black drapery and the embellishments all around, and on the faces and beards... [of] the prophets who are on the wall above the well (i.e., above the baptismal font)". Although much altered, the first three prophets appear to have been produced by the workshop of the Master of St Gaggio, which is responsible also for the busts on the preceding walls, while the softer and more voluminous figures of the next three prophets were probably done later by an artist more strongly influenced by Giotto.

After the interruption of the east wall – which, as we have seen, lost its mosaics during the 18th century – the series of busts continues along the north-east wall with *Solomon, David, Malachi, Zechariah,*

On the parapet of the south-west section, also restored recently, are busts of the Prophets and Patriarchs Moses, Jacob, Isaac, Abraham, Enoch *and* Elijah. *These "plutei" were done around 1310 and have been ascribed to artists working in conjunction with the Master of San Gaggio.*

Haggai and *Zephanaiah*, all of them marred by excessive restoration. A cautious guess would be that these mosaics are Florentine work of the first two decades of the 14th century.

On the north wall are busts of *Habakkuk, Nahum, Micah, Jonas, Obadiah* and *Amos*. In comparison to the busts in the south part of the building, these figures (also over-restored) are freer and more varied in movement, suggesting that they belong to a later time and style. *Obadiah* and *Amos* especially – in particular the latter's head – have points in common with the scene of the *Lamentation* on the dome. This was one of the last scenes of the great cycle to be executed, and may be attributed to Lippo di Bienivieni, who is also the probable author of two further busts of prophets and other figures on the adjacent wall (see below).

On the north-west wall are *Joel, Hosea, Ezekiel, Daniel, Jeremiah* and *Isaiah*, all of them restored by Alessio Baldovinetti. In the spring of 1489 the painter noted down in his memoirs that he was paid 19 florins for renovating the mosaics situated "above the tomb of Pope Ioanni (i.e. Pope John XXIII)", whose funeral monument rests against this wall. The mosaics have undoubtedly undergone heavy alteration, but, like the preceding ones on the north wall, they are marked by a greater original fluidity and modernity than the mosaics on the south walls. This leads us to suppose that the busts on this seventh wall – where *Ezekiel* and *Jeremiah* are decidedly in the Gothic-Giottesque style of Lippo di Bienivieni – were probably among the last to have been executed.

The Architraves Above the Portals

Original sources suggest that after 1325 no further mosaic decoration was attempted in the Baptistery for a century and a half. In the second half of the 1400s, this technique – which at the time was being rediscovered by Florentine artists – was again used to decorate the architraves above the two portals filled by Ghiberti's sets of doors. The south portal had already been given mosaics (see p. 107) in the early 14th century, when a second wave of such decoration was extended to the areas below the dome. The filling of the east portal with the Gates of Paradise was seen as an opportunity to complete the old mosaic project for the architraves. To this purpose, Alessio Baldovinetti – a skillful mosaicist as well as a renowned painter – set to work on the architrave of the north portal, which after 1453 was fitted with Ghib-

Alessio Baldovinetti authored this mosaic on the intrados of the architrave of the north portal. Dating from 1453, it shows the face of St John the Baptist encircled by three acanthus coils and flanked by two tetramorphic (i.e. "four-shaped") figures. In the Old Testament the Prophet Ezechiel describes these creatures as blending the traits of man, ox, lion and eagle: they foreshadow the fabulous beasts mentioned by the Evangelists.

erti's first set of bronze doors. In 1455, the architrave of the east portal was also mosaicked. This medium must have appeared to contemporaries as a fitting complement to such superb doors, but its choice was surely also dictated by a wish to establish a decorative continuity within the Baptistery. At that time the mosaic technique was very popular in Florence, thanks to the work done by Baldovinetti and by Domenico and David Ghirlandaio's workshop.

Baldovinetti executed a traditional composition for the architrave of the north portal. This consists of a central head of St John the Baptist, flanked by two tetramorphic figures and contained within a pattern of acanthus leaves. It echoes the 14th-century mosaic decorating the architrave above the Pisano doors. Although restoration has altered it – in particular the figure of St John – the work is not distinguished for any particular creativity, and the technique still lacks assurance.

Two years later, when Baldovinetti did the mosaic on the architrave of the east door, his style had matured and become more complex. Here, two full-length figures of angels rest on a cloud and hold a garland of flowers over the head of Christ. The compositional scheme is rooted in classicism, and inspired by the well-known subject of winged genii holding a *clipeus*. The angels are eloquent examples in the mosaic medium of the pictorial canons of those times, and appear particularly influenced – in terms of types and drapery – by Andrea del Castagno, although Baldovinetti here interprets that master's style with the "dry and somewhat unpolished" manner which Vasari reproached him for. The unusual depiction of a beardless Christ appears to hark back to early Christian prototypes, which also inspired Baldovinetti's technique of mosaic setting. This is based on a loose arrangement of the tesserae, which helps to make the figures visible from a distance.

Baldovinetti later devoted himself to the restoration of the mosaics in the Baptistery, and in 1481 was employed here permanently, up to his death in 1499. From 1487 on, he left a number of cursory references in his *Ricordi* concerning this work.

Appendix: Baptistery Furnishings at the Opera del Duomo Museum

While over the centuries the Baptistery's interior was enriched with a wealth of beautiful artistic objects and furnishings, it also underwent a number of wrenching transformations, which have meant the loss of a significant part of its artistic heritage. The pieces that have survived are today at the Opera del Duomo Museum, which houses all the art produced for the Cathedral, Campanile and Baptistery.

Sculptures

Two Roman Sarcophagi
Of the many sarcophagi dating from Roman times which were re-used as tombs and left to dot the square outside the Baptistery, two still stood at either side of Andrea Pisano's doors until a short time ago. The first is a sarcophagus with columns, with wedding scenes carved on three of its sides. The front panel depicts at the centre a man and a woman being united in marriage by joining each other's right hand (*dextrarum iunctio*). To the left of the main

scene is the bridegroom dressed in military clothes, and to the right is the bride, a veil covering her head. On the two short sides, the right panel shows a bearded captive surrendering to an officer, while on the left panel a priest takes a bull to be sacrificed. From the reliefs it appears that the sarcophagus dates from the 2nd century AD. The lid, which is sloped on two sides and decorated with tiles in fish-scale pattern, evidently belongs to another sarcophagus, for its underside does not fit properly into the opening.

The second stone coffin dates from the same period. The front panel is decorated with what appears to be a funeral scene. At the centre, Mercury is seen coming out of the door of Hades. A niche on either side contains the figures of two women. The heads of both are carved in a different marble and style from the rest of the relief: the additions were probably made when the coffin was used again as a tomb. Each side panel depicts a griffon in low relief.

The Old Baptismal Font
The surviving pieces of what once was the 13th-century baptismal font are both historically and artistically significant. The basin, which for three centuries represented the living heart of the Baptistery, was torn down in 1577 by Bernardo Buontalenti (see p. 21). In the 16th century the Baptistery was believed to be a Roman temple, and the medieval font was seen as disrupting the spatial effect of its interior. On these grounds Vincenzo Borghini, a scholar in the service of the Medici ruler who ordered the font demolished, wrote in critical terms that "the font at the centre strongly disfigures (the building's interior), since taking up the space in the middle makes it appear smaller by half". The opinion of the intellectual circles of the time was far removed from the simple attachment of the people of Florence to the basin in which they and all their forbears had been baptized. The feeling was so strong that after the font was broken up and

dumped near the city walls, many Florentines chipped small pieces off the marble slabs to cherish as holy relics.

The thirty-one extant fragments now housed in Opera del Duomo were all recovered fortuitously. The main rescue operation took place in 1905, after some of the slabs were discovered during renovation of the Baptistery roof. They bore an inscription attesting that they had been moved there in 1749. Other pieces were dug up around the base of the pilasters of the *scarsella*, while further pieces surfaced during excavations in the surrounding square. These fragments are not sufficient to allow us to make a reliable reconstruction of the original font. According to the drawing that its demolisher Bernardo Buontalenti made of it, the font had eight sides and was linked to the altar in the *scarsella* by an enclosure. Like other 13th-century baptismal fonts surviving here and there in Tuscany, this one too may have been equipped with small basins along its inside walls, in which to immerse the individuals to be christened.

There is disagreement among historians as to the font's date of execution, which is based on the stylistic features of the surviving slabs. The general opinion, however, is that it was made in the first quarter of the 13th century. It was probably set up when the *scarsella* and the Baptistery floor were renovated – sometime between 1201 and 1225. Although the slabs differ in design, they all have in common an exclusively abstract decorative scheme, with various geometrical patterns done in white and green marble, together with sections in relief carved into the white marble slabs. This ornamental scheme dates from the second half of the 13th century, and is originally Pisan: from Pisa it spread to Lucca, Pistoia and Florence, where we find it embellishing not only the enclosures of the Baptistery's baptismal font and choir, but also the presbytery in San Miniato al Monte (early 13th century).

The Statues that once Stood above the Portals

In the 16th century other important sculptural ornaments dating from the Baptistery's medieval phase were likewise removed and in part lost. We are left today with mere pieces of the statues that once stood over the portals. The Sienese Tino di Camaino sculpted

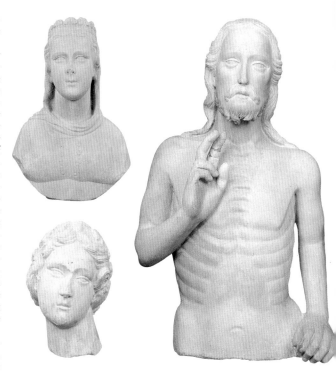

The surviving fragments of Tino di Camaino's sculptures, now at the Opera del Duomo Museum, include the bust of Faith *and the head of* Hope *(left, from top) which flanked the statue of St John on the east side of the Baptistery. The* Christ Raising His Hand in Blessing *(right) was part of the group on the south wall.*

them around 1330. Three mutilated marble fragments – a bust, a half-length figure and a head – belonging to three female figures portraying *Faith, Charity* and *Hope* respectively, are what remains of the statuary Tino did for the east doors during his last stay in Florence, where they used to stand beside a statue of St John the Baptist which has also been lost. The three Theological Virtues were often coupled with the figure of St John the Baptist, as attested by their presence at the foot of the *Beheading of St John the Baptist*, a bronze group authored by Vincenzo Danti in the second half of the 16th century (see p. 29) for the south doors. In earlier times, this portal had been surmounted by a marble group portraying the *Baptism of Christ*. Of this group only the head of *St John the Baptist* and a bust of *Christ Raising His Hand in Blessing* have come down to us. They were discovered in 1844 in the courtyard of the presbytery adjoining the Baptistery. From contemporary paint-

ings we know that the group included an angel, and that all three images stood inside pinnacled niches.

The Wooden Crucifix

Another significant 14th-century sculpture associated with the Baptistery is the painted wooden *Crucifix* which stood atop an altar on the right of the Gates of Paradise for just under six centuries (1333 to 1912). Due to the intense and uninterrupted worship of the Crucifix, the altar was transformed time and again. The last version, in marble, dates from 1741, and was demolished during the 1898-1908 restoration program. The veneration for the old wooden Christ on the Cross stemmed from the belief that it had been carved out of the elm which allegedly stood in the Cathedral square in early times, and which had flowered by miracle when the coffin containing the deceased Bishop Zenobius passed by. The arms of the Christ, which were once fitted into the trunk so that they could be moved, were

(1676-1745) had constructed it with coloured marble inlays in 1732 to replace the previous altar, which had been demolished the year before. It was surmounted by a sizable group of statues portraying *St John the Baptist Carried in Glory by Two Angels*, and two additional angels standing on either side of the group bearing torches. Ticciati had also inserted five marble reliefs of *Stories of St John the Baptist* (at Opera del Duomo). On the antependium was *St John the Baptist's Head is Presented to Herod* – the scene immediate-

The Museum also houses a number of furnishings which at one time embellished the Baptistery's interior. These include a polychrome wooden Crucifix, carved by a Tuscan artist around the mid 14th century, and the image of Mary Magdalen, a celebrated example of Donatello's mature style, painstakingly restored after the 1966 flood.

at a later date fastened along the sides of the body in harmony with the accepted model of Christ in scenes of the *Deposition*. Recent renovation brought the arms back to their original position, and restored the statue's original colours, so that we can now admire its high artistic quality. Attributed by some scholars to Andrea Pisano, the Crucifix is undoubtedly the creation of a great and refined artist of the early 14th century.

Donatello's Mary Magdalen

Another masterpiece of wooden statuary is Donatello's *Mary Magdalen*. It is known to have been in the Baptistery as early as 1500, and was probably intended for this location from the very start. Although the image was moved more than once from one spot to another inside the building, it was always a much-admired work. This is attested by a 1731 inscription, put up when the statue was placed on an altar on the left of the Gates of Paradise (demolished in the early 20th century). We are struck

by the ascetic and expressive figure of the repentant Mary Magdalen, "emaciated by fasting and self-denial", as Vasari put it. The memory of her past beauty is evoked by the golden streaks in her hair, which covers her like a garment. The dramatic spiritual tension and the quasi-expressionistic outlines of her figure belong to Donatello's late manner. He probably carved his *Mary Magdalen* some time before Neri di Bicci did his own rendition of the subject in 1455, for the latter is strongly influenced by Donatello's image.

The 18th-Century High Altar

During the Renaissance and Baroque periods there was little hesitation to transform the 'old-fashioned' interior of the Baptistery. The purist 1898-1908 restoration campaign tried instead to annul all post-medieval alterations and return the building to its 'original' appearance. In 1912 the marble high altar was removed from the *scarsella*. The Florentine sculptor Girolamo Ticciati

ly following the dance of Salome and the beheading of the Saint. The other four reliefs were inside medallions placed at regular intervals on the semi-circular balustrade enclosing the altar. They represent, in chronological order: the *Visitation, Zechariah Blesses the Young John before he Sets Out for the Desert; Ecce Agnus Dei (Behold the Lamb of God)* and *St John the Baptist Before Herod.* The group included four eagles, emblems of the Calimala guild. Two eagles were portrayed in the round, holding up the mensa, while the other two in high relief stood between the medallions on the balustrade. The group – which we can only appreciate from the photographs taken before the altar was broken up – had a theatrical Baroque air about it, yet the style of the sculptures – and of the reliefs as well – was a good example of 18th-century Florentine art, itself modelled on Renaissance sculpture in general and Baccio Bandinelli's work in particular.

Gold-Work

Altar of St John the Baptist
Amongst the many surpassing examples of gold-work which over the centuries came to enrich the Baptistery Treasury, the finest and most celebrated is the altar of St John the Baptist. This extraordinary object shaped like a parallelepiped consists of cast sections and enamelled ones, and is made of chased and engraved silver. It took more than a century to complete (*circa* 1366-1483).

Thanks to this, it appears to us today as a highly qualified synthesis of Florentine sculpture and the goldsmith's craft as it developed from the Gothic period into the full Renaissance.

Eight Gothic pilasters with a polygonal base divide the altar on three sides into twelve compartments – eight on the front and two on each side – containing reliefs of the life of St John the Baptist. The upper portion of the altar is lined by a series of niches containing

statues of *Saints, Prophets* and *Sybils.* Originally there were ninety-five figures, but loss and theft have brought this number down to eighty-two. On the front portion of the altar, at the centre, inside a niche surmounted by small figures of prophets, is a large figure in the round of St John the Baptist. Eight scenes from his life are represented here. On the left of the niche, starting from the top, are, the *Baptism of Christ, Christ Visits St John in the Wilderness, St*

John the Baptist Preaches to the Crowds and *The Youthful St John Leaves His Family and Goes into the Wilderness*. On the right, *St John the Baptist Before Herod, Baptism of the Crowds, Christ Receives the Messengers of St John the Baptist* and *The Disciples Visit St John the Baptist in Prison*. On the left-hand side of the altar are scenes from the early life of the Saint: *Announcement to Zechariah and the Visitation*, and *Birth of St John the Baptist*. On the right-hand side are the final episodes: *Beheading of St John the Baptist* and *St John the Baptist's Head Is Presented to Herod*.

The launching of the project to build the altar is mentioned in an inscription on a strip of enamel running across the foot of the altar: ANNO DOMINI 1366 INCEPTUM FUIT HOC OPUS DOSSALIS TEMPORIS NEROZZI DE ALBERTIS MICHAELIS DE RONDINELLIS BERNARDI DOMINI DE CHOVONIBUS DEPUTATORUM ("This frontal was commenced in the year of Our Lord 1336, in the time of Benedetto Nerozzo degli Alberti, Paolo Michele dei Rondinelli, Bernardo son of Covone de' Covoni, appointed officials"). Florence had only recently shaken off the Great Plague, which for some years brought everyday business and life to a grinding halt. In 1364 it prevailed over Pisa, thus gaining a port on the Mediterranean Sea. Once again, Florence's economic recovery went hand in hand with renewed activity in the arts, which now came to include this remarkable *ex voto*, offered up to the city's patron Saint.

Two years after work had started on the altar, Arte di Calimala made the first payments to Betto di Geri and Leonardo di Ser Giovanni, two goldsmiths who had joined the venture. The latter is thought to have had a primary role in designing the reliefs. Further payments were made in 1377 and 1378 to Michele di Monte and Cristofano di Paolo, but the vouchers do not specify what sections of the altar were done by each. We do know, however, that between 1445 and 1452, Tommaso, the son of the great Lorenzo Ghiberti, and Matteo di Giovanni, were working on the central niche, and that Michelozzo, a former member of Donatello's workshop, did the statuette in the round of St John the Baptist.

The altar was completed at the end of the 15th century, after pooling the painstaking efforts of a host of gold-

smiths and the devotion of an entire city. It attracted the participation of some of the most important Florentine sculptors of the time. Antonio del Pollaiolo and Bernardo Cennini authored the *Birth of St John the Baptist* and the *Announcement to Zechariah* on the altar's left side, while the two reliefs on the right side (1477-1483) are by Andrea del Verrocchio, Antonio Salvi and Francesco di Giovanni.

We can assume that the original design was not for a proper altar, but for a frontal, or antependium, to be placed in front of the high altar during important functions. At a later date this was turned into a full-scale altar, to display the Treasury of San Giovanni during all festivities linked to Florence's patron Saint. In 1475 a letter written by the humanist Pietro Cennini confirms that in his time the silver altar was used as a monstrance, to be held up to the admiring gaze of the faithful, resting on the old baptismal font. The custom of displaying the altar from a higher level, at the centre of the building, persisted till after the middle of the 18th century, long after the removal of the old baptismal font which had served as a prop for it. During the siege of 1529, which put Florence's endurance to a severe test, the altar was brought out on the square between the Baptistery and the Cathedral, to instill a warlike spirit into the citizen army. Here the assembled soldiery swore a solemn oath to defend the city. During its public displays, which continued till the end of the 19th century, the altar was dressed up with a glittering mass of objects from the Treasury of San Giovanni, including censers, chalices, candelabra, reliquaries, crosses and the like. Many of these can still be seen today in the museum.

15th-century Casket Inlaid with Semi-Precious Stones
Amongst the works exposed to the veneration of the faithful, was a shrine shaped like an ark. According to the scholar Anton Francesco Gori, in 1749 it was one of a pair of caskets placed on the altar of St John the Baptist. This sparkling object is made of silver, in part gold-plated and encrusted with an array of multi-coloured semi-precious stones, arranged in lozenge shapes on the sides and in scales on the sloping lid. Some authorities have connected the shrine to a payment made in 1476 to

Vittore Ghiberti, son of Lorenzo, for the construction of "a reliquary box for Santa Maria del Fiore". Its date of execution, tentatively placed around the late 1400s, seems to be confirmed by the the acanthus leaves ending in lions' paws with outstretched claws, which decorate the corners. This classical motif is modelled on Verrocchio's popular Medici sarcophagus, now in the sacristy of the church of San Lorenzo.

Portable Mosaic Depicting the Twelve Major Christian Holidays
This precious small mosaic was donated in 1394 to the Baptistery Treasury by the Venetian lady Nicoletta Grioni, widow of the son of an official of the Imperial court in Constantinople. It consists of two panels, at one time

hinged together to form a small portable altar. The mosaic is an exquisite example of the artistic quality and technical perfection achieved by Byzantine art in the 14th century. The twelve scenes are done with minute tesserae – gold leaf for the backgrounds and vitreous paste for the figures – set in a shallow bed of wax. The execution is of such masterly quality that it is hard to imagine how such subtly pictorial effects could have been achieved without the use of a paintbrush, but simply by putting together tiny mosaic pieces with an exquisite sense of colour. The scenes are enclosed within two turns of an ornamental fascia, itself a refined work in gold leaf and chased silver enamel. To allow such a delicate object to be put on display, the 15th-century consuls of Arte di Calimala set the two mosaic panels within a gilded frame. The guild's emblem, an eagle clawing a torsello, or bale of wool, has been painted on the back of the frame.

Anichino Corsi's Ex Voto

Another token of devotion presented to the Baptistery Treasury is Anichino Corsi's *ex voto*. This consists of a large, many-armed coral branch shooting out of a cluster of silver leaves, supported by a partly gilded silver base. The base is interrupted at the centre by a large, spherical knot, which bears a Latin inscription dedicating to St John the Baptist this object, "wrested from the spoils of the Moors". The coral branch, precious in its own right, was considered all the more valuable for having been snatched from the Muslims. In 1447 Arte di Calimala commissioned "Rinaldo di Giovanni di Ghino and his partners, goldsmiths" to fashion the costly setting for this *ex voto*.

Reliquary of the Arm of St Philip and Other Saints

Much of the Treasury of San Giovanni was once made up of reliquaries. The surviving pieces are highly representative of the quality of gold work done in the past for the Baptistery.

The reliquary containing St Philip's arm comprises two parts dating from different periods. The bone of the Saint's arm is housed in the upper section, in a glass cylinder set within a frame of gilded silver which has the shape of a small temple surmounted by a dome. Records indicate that the relic

was donated by Monaco de' Corbizzi, a Florentine cleric who became Chancellor of the Patriarch of Jerusalem and returned to Florence from the Holy Land in 1204. The lower section of the reliquary contains the relics of a number of other saints. Made of gilded silver, it has the shape of a six-sided urn, with glass panels to make the relics visible. An inscription in Gothic characters round the base tells us that these relics (another gift of the Venetian noblewoman Nicoletta Grioni) arrived from Constantinople in 1394 and were placed inside this reliquary four years later. The style of this anonymous work is both simple and refined, and seems to agree with the date mentioned in the inscription.

The temple-shaped upper section is structurally in tune with late Gothic taste. Its buttresses are decorated with statuettes of prophets. It is later in date than the lower portion, and may be the work of the goldsmith Antonio di Pietro del Vagliente, according to a document of 1425. The fine statuette in the round of St Philip which surmounts the reliquary is the work of another artist. The strong Donatello-like lines of this figure suggest that its author could be Michelozzo, the partner of the great sculptor and a goldsmith as well.

Reliquary of the Finger of St John the Baptist

The Opera del Duomo Museum conserves two reliquaries which go under this name. The one that comes from the Baptistery houses a relic which, according to Bishop Antonino, was brought back from Constantinople in 1392 by Pepo di Arnaldo di Lapo Ruspi. The object, dating from the 15th century, is made of finely chased gold and gilded copper. The circular temple containing the relic stands on top of an exquisitely wrought stem with a multifoil base. In the 18th century it was refurbished – maybe by Bernardo Holzman, the goldsmith who in 1723 was entrusted with restoring this and all the other reliquaries in the Baptistery. On the cupola stands a cast silver statue of St John the Baptist.

Reliquary of St Simeon the Stylite

Made of silver and gilded copper, this object is actually composed of two separate reliquaries. The lower part, in the shape of a six-sided silver urn with transparent crystal panels, contains relics, which according to an inscription on the base were donated to the Baptistery by Charlemagne and placed inside this casket in 1398. The upper part is shaped like a candelabrum and embossed with decorative designs, including the Calimala emblem. At the top is a cylindrical crystal casket to display other relics. The upper part probably dates from the late 1400s, but the reliquary has since then undergone a number of alterations and refurbishings. For example, the six small lions, which according to old documents stood at the corners of the six-sided base, have been replaced with Baroque volutes.

Reliquary of the Libretto

The 'Libretto' Reliquary also consists of two parts, each of which has its own history. One is the 'Libretto' proper, which contains relics of the Passion and was at all times highly venerated. The second part is a reliquary in the shape of a miniature temple, created at a later date to contain the former. In 1501 the goldsmith Giovanni Sogliani completed this latter object, which is considered to be his masterpiece. It is an architectural view of remarkable elegance, supported by a quatrefoil pedestal with the Calimala eagle. The niche containing the 'Libretto' is made of gilded silver and enamel, and is embellished with both decorative details and figures. It ends in a classical tympanum with statuettes in the round portraying St John the Baptist at the summit, eagles on the lintel and two kneeling angels holding up the 'Libretto'.

The 'Libretto' itself is a small polyptych in gold and enamel, studded with rubies and pearls. Its seventy-two panels, shaped like mullioned windows with one light, contain the relics. The work is a rare and wonderful example of late-14th-century French art. In the central area is a scroll illuminated on both sides, with a *Crucifixion* and the *Trinity* between the portraits of Charles V of France and his wife Jeanne de Bourbon. A French inscription states that King Charles presented this reliquary to his brother Louis, Duke of Anjou, who died in Italy in 1384. In 1465 the coveted object was in the private collection of Piero de' Medici (the Gouty), after which it went to Lorenzo the Magnificent. Arte di Calimala purchased it in 1495 and placed it in the Baptistery Treasury.

Reliquary of St John the Baptist's Jaw

This casket is made of silver and partly gilded copper and is shaped like a miniature temple with a central plan, standing atop a tall stem with a double knot. The temple containing the relic is the most elaborate part of the object. It is domed, surrounded by six diminutive columns, and its sides are made of glass panels. Its elegant appearance is completed by six angels in the round and a full length figure of St John the Baptist at the top. The Reliquary of St John the Baptist's Jaw is yet another gift to the Baptistery by Nicoletta Grioni in 1394. The case it rested in initially was replaced in 1564 by the present casket, crafted by Pietro Cerluzi for Cosimo I de' Medici. No other works have been attributed to this goldsmith, but on the strength of this single piece he can immediately be proclaimed as one of Giambologna's most important pupils.

Reliquary of St John the Baptist's Index Finger

This reliquary in Baroque style is made of cast silver and semi-precious stones. Enveloped in an intricate array of plant motifs and cherubim heads, it ends with a niche surmounted by a statuette depicting the Agnus Dei. An inscription at the base of the shrine records that it was fashioned in 1698 and financed by the Florentine nobleman Francesco Maria Sergrifi.

Mention is made of an earlier shrine of gold, silver and pearls, to house St John the Baptist's index finger. This was a gift made by Baldassarre Cossa (Antipope John XXIII) to the Republic of Florence.

Antonio del Pollaiolo's Silver Cross

As monumental in its proportions as it is exquisite in its fashioning, this masterpiece of the goldsmith's craft was produced by the Florentine Renaissance and is celebrated far and wide.

The object comprises a cross and an elaborate stand. The latter is also of silver, and on its large multifoliate base rest two harpies who are seen holding up a pair of adoring angels. Here, the knot on the stem takes on the form of a classical domed temple with a hexagonal plan, with niches containing statuettes in the round of St John the Baptist and angels. Above, two volutes spring up from the stem and act as a support for figures in the round depicting the *Mourners*.

The cross is carved on both sides. The front shows a cast silver Christ in the round. The spectacular ensemble is completed by a series of enamels portraying holy figures and some allegories. Here the outstanding pictorial skills of Antonio del Pollaiolo very much match his prowess as a goldsmith and sculptor.

In 1457 Arte di Calimala commissioned three artists (Betto di Francesco, Antonio del Pollaiolo and Miliano Dei) to fashion "a great silver cross". According to contemporary documents, the job was completed as early as 1459, but other sources suggest that Pollaiolo was still working on the cross in 1468. This discrepancy has led some historians to suppose that the object, originally designed as a reliquary, was later given the monumental stand with which it is associated today. The ensemble is intended to celebrate St John the Baptist, the Forerunner of Christ.

Vestments with Scenes from the Life of St John the Baptist

Antonio del Pollaiolo can also be credited with the pictorial project for the celebrated vestments of St John the Baptist. As prescribed by the solemn liturgy for high mass, the vestments include a cope, a chasuble and two under-habits, decorated with gold embroidery and multicoloured silk, depicting scenes from the life of this saint.

As early as the 18th century the gold and white brocade of the vestments were frayed beyond recognition. Nevertheless, twenty-seven embroidered squares survive to this day. Far from being a minor work, the cloth may, in terms of stylistic quality and iconographic expertise, be counted amongst the most significant artistic monuments of 15th-century Florentine art.

The embroidery – "a punto serrato", as Vasari described it, or *or nué* – consists of very close and very tiny stitches, conjuring pictorial modulations so subtle as to be indistinguishable from a true painting. This overall effect was imparted to the cloth not only by Pollaiolo's constant supervision, but also thanks to the embroiderers' stunning technical prowess, which Vasari ascribes chiefly to Paolo da Verona, "divine in that profession". Nevertheless, a number of different craftsmen are known to have worked on the object from 1466 to 1488. Some of these, such as Piero di Piero da Venezia and Antonio di Giovanni da Firenze, were Italian, while others were Spanish, French (Nicholas of Jacob) and Flemish (John of Malines and Paul of Antwerp). The munificent merchants of Arte di Calimala forked out no less than 3179 gold florins to cover its cost.

Opificio delle Pietre Dure has recently launched a program to restore this priceless work of embroidery. The task promises to be delicate and time-consuming. Indeed, it is through this effort of conservation that we can measure the loving devotion that the city of Florence continues to have for the Baptistery and its treasures.

The Vestments of St John the Baptist portray the life of this saint with an unrivalled wealth of details. Below, from left to right and from the top down: six of the surviving twenty-seven pieces: The Visitation; Birth of St John the Baptist; Zechariah Writes Down John's Name; The Circumcision; St John Meets the Customs Officials; St John Meets the High Priest. The design on the cloth is executed with a technique that makes the closely-spaced and minute stitches well-nigh invisible. Completed in 1487, after twenty-two years of painstaking labour, this clerical garment tells us an enormous amount about the artistic development of the cartoons' author. Antonio del Pollaiolo, who became the acknowledged master for a whole generation of artists, devised a new set of spatial rules and ventured well beyond the "courtly" style of the early Renaissance as represented by Benozzo Gozzoli.

Glossary

abacus (Lat. *abacus*, from the Gk. *ábax*, 'tablet') the uppermost member of a capital.

acanthus a plant whose large, deeply indented leaves inspired the typical ornamentation of the Corinthian capital*.

aedicule → niche.

angelic choirs these include the Old Testament Cherubim and Seraphim and the seven other ranks into which theologians classify angels.

antependium → frontal.

apse (from the Gk. *hápsos*, 'articulation') a structure that is semicircular or polygonal in plan, and vaulted. In general, its form is discernible from the exterior. In Christian basilicas the main apse terminates the nave and coincides with the presbytery*.

arch a curved structure spanning a light* (as of a door, window or bridge). It distributes the thrust of pressure from above onto the vertical structures supporting it. When an arch's radius is equal to its height, it is called a round arch. If the radius is less, it is a pointed, or ogee, arch. When the radius is greater, we speak of a depressed arch. A blind arch is walled (i.e., without an opening), while the rampant arch – typical of the Gothic style – is asymmetrical and acts as a buttress.

architrave a horizontal member that connects two vertical structural members and carries the weight of the upper structure; a part of the entablature that rests on the capitals* and is directly below the frieze*.

archivolt surface or moulding around an arch.

arriccio an Italian term designating the layer of rough plaster upon which the artist copied a preliminary drawing, or cartoon*. An additional fine layer of plaster was then spread over this.

Atlas → telamon.

base the lower part of an isolated structural member, such as a pillar* or a column*.

bas-relief → relief.

bestiary a medieval allegorical treatise which describes different animals and endows them with human virtues and vices; also, medieval sculptural decoration based on such works.

buttress a structure of masonry for supporting walls exerting strong horizontal pressure.

capital (Lat. *caput*, 'head') the part connecting a vertical structural member (such as a column*, pillar* or pilaster strip*) to the overhead structure. The Doric capital has the shape of an abacus*, or square slab, and a rounded echinus*; the Ionic capital is characterized by spiral volutes*, while the Corinthian capital is enveloped in acanthus* leaves.

cartoon a preliminary drawing for a fresco, mosaic or tapestry. In the fresco technique, holes are punched along

the contours of the drawing and sprinkled with lampblack, after which the artist traces the drawing in sinopia* mixed with water.

centering a framework supporting an arch or vault while these are under construction.

chasing in this specific context, the term has been used to designate a finishing technique for metal objects. After the casting process, the medieval or Renaissance artist employed a *punzone* – or four-sided trimming tool that tapers at the edges – to embellish the object with further ornamental work.

chasuble in the Catholic church, a loose vestment open on the sides, worn over the alb by priests at ceremonies.

cipolin → marble.

clipeus a Latin term, designating a large round copper shield used by Roman soldiers.

column a vertical member with a round shaft, for support or decoration. Classical Greek architecture lists three orders of columns. The Doric column is without a base and has a massive shaft that tapers* at the top. It is decorated with twenty vertical grooves. The Ionic column rests on a round base, and its elongated and tapering shaft with twenty-four grooves is often hewn out of a monolith. The Corinthian column is a variation of the Ionic (→ order).

compasso a 15th-century Italian term for a mixtilinear* frame or other decoration, typical of the Gothic style.

cope vestment worn by priests consisting of a large open cloak fastened at the height of the breast with a clip.

coretto small recessed areas in a church, with an opening (often covered by a grate) from which one can follow a religious service without being seen.

diptych (Gk. *di-*, 'two' + *ptússo*, 'fold') a picture or pictures on two tablets (three in the triptych) that are hinged together. A polyptych consists of four or more hinged and folding tablets.

drum an upright wall between a building and the dome that crowns it.

echinus (Gk. *ekhînos*, 'serpent') the lowermost part, or bell, of a capital* of a column*.

elevation the vertical section of a building.

embossing in this specific context, technique of modelling figures on a metal plate which consists of applying pressure on the underside to raise the surface.

extrados the curved external surface of an arch.

festoon an ornamental motif of classical origin consisting of a string of flowers or leaves hanging in a curve between two points.

flabellum Latin term for a fan made of leaves or feathers.

fresco a technique of wall painting which uses earth pigments thinned with water and applied on freshly-spread wet plaster. The ensuing chemical reaction between slaked lime and carbon dioxide in the air forms a calcium carbonate film that fixes the colours.

frieze a horizontal – often decorated – member of the entablature, between the architrave* and the cornice. Any ornamental horizontal band on a building.

frontal an ornamental covering of cloth or other material for the front of an altar.

gargoyle a spout projecting over the edge or corner of a building to discharge rainwater clear of the external walls. Gargoyles often have the form of a grotesque human figure or animal.

gilding to apply a thin layer of gold on a metal surface. Methods of doing this include gold-plating, gilding with gold leaf, and applying gold and mercury amalgam. Another process is by galvanization, in which electrolysis leaves a thin film of gold oxide on the surface.

gnomon (Gk. *gnòmon*) a pointer on a sundial indicating the time of day by the position of its shadow.

griffon griffon vulture; also a winged monster used as a decorative element in art.

grotesque fantastic decorative element consisting of masks, winged fish, leaves and others. The term derives from the ancient name of *Domus Aurea*'s ruins in Rome, "the grottoes".

harpy a mythological animal with the body of a bird and the head of a woman, which dragged the dead to Hades.

hemicycle (Gk. *hemi-*, 'half' + *kúklos*, 'circle') part of a building forming a semicircular structure.

impost a surface on which an arch or vault rests; a member projecting from a jamb or pilaster from which an arch springs.

inlay a decorative pattern or design inserted on a wooden or marble (or other) surface by using geometric shapes made from the same or other materials.

intrados the curved internal surface of an arch.

lantern (Gk. *lamptèr*) uppermost member of a dome or tower with a circular or polygonal plant, having glazed sides for admission of light.

lesene a pilaster* with a predominantly decorative function that projects only slightly from the wall.

light opening in a wall or roof, or the space between the mullions of a window (→ mullioned window).

lorica a light cuirass used by the Romans.

lozenge a diamond-shaped decorative element.

lunette an opening at the top of a wall, under an arch or rounded part of a wall, often decorated with a fresco or mosaic; also the uppermost part of an altarpiece.

Luni marble white marble quarried at Luni, near Carrara.

marble a stone employed for ornamental or architectural purposes, capable of taking a high polish. The inlays that decorate the Baptistery in Florence include not only Carrara white marble and cipolin, a white-and-green marble that flakes easily, but also the green-mottled Prato serpentine stone.

medallion a decorative motif consisting of a painted figure or one in relief, set inside a round or oval frame.

mixtilinear any figure made of straight and curved lines.

monstrance a vessel in which the Host is exposed for veneration.

mortar a mixture of sand, water and a binder (e.g. lime), used as a building material.

moulding a decorative projection running between two parts of a building.

mullioned window a window with vertical divisions (such as a colonnette or pillar). They may have one, two, or more lights*.

multifoil a figure or frame with a number of curving sides or lobes – trefoil or quatrefoil when they are three or four. A trefoil is also an arch* composed of three lobes.

nave the longitudinal part of a church, defined by the exterior walls or by rows of columns or pillars. The term derives from the Greek *naus*, 'ship', which in early Christian times was used as a metaphor for a place of worship.

niche a recess in a wall, similar to a shrine. Often shaped like the front of a temple, and supported by columns or pillars. A similar free-standing structure is called an aedicule or pavilion.

oculus a circular opening in a building.

"opus signinum" a material for paving floors made by mixing pieces of crushed brick with resin or lime.

order in architectural context, the two members (column* and entablature*) which are proportioned and decorated in accordance with a prescribed architectural mode (e.g. Doric, Ionian, Corinthian).

ornament any sculpture, carving, painting and stuccoes having a mainly decorative purpose.

pavilion roof (Lat. *papilio*, 'butterfly') rectangular-shaped roof with four sloping sides.

parapet a low protective wall at the edge of a terrace, window and the like.

pier an upright structural member supporting an arch* or lintel.

pilaster supporting member that is different from a column in that it is rectangular or otherwise in plan.

pilaster strip → lesene.

plinth (Gk. *plínthos*, 'brick') a square or polygonal base upon which a column or pillar rests.

presbytery (Gk. *presbutèrion*, 'council of elders') the area of a church surrounding the high altar. Usually raised and enclosed by a railing, it is reserved for the clergy during a religious function.

relief sculptural work in which the figures project from a background. In a high relief, the figures project by more than half their thickness. The projection is much less in the case of a low relief, and negligible in the *stiacciato* ('flattened out') relief, where it decreases gradually from the foreground to the background, thus creating an illusion of depth. 'In the round' designates a fully sculptured figure visible from all sides.

rib a curving member that reinforces vaults and domes, but is sometimes purely decorative.

rose window circular window on the façade of Gothic or Romanesque churches, chapels and others, to bring more light to the nave. Often in the shape of a rose or wheel.

rosette a circular decoration with a central button surrounded by foliage and flower motifs.

sandstone sedimentary rock united by a cement of sandy composition. *Pietra serena*, used in Tuscany in medieval and Renaissance architecture, is a form of sandstone.

"scarsella" a rectangular apse*.

scroll a roll of paper or parchment with writing on it.

serpentine stone → marble.

singing gallery part of a church occupied by the singers. In Italian churches this is often an elevated loggia containing the organ as well.

sinopia preliminary drawing made directly on the wall, for mosaics and frescoes. The word derives from Sinope, a Greek city on the Black Sea which in ancient times produced the red ochre pigment used for this purpose.

splay an opening in a wall with oblique sides. Doors or windows with slanting sides – opening outward or inward – are splayed.

"stiacciato" technique → relief.

stud a round-headed knob or nail used for protection and/or ornament.

tapering progressive narrowing toward one end of the cross section of a column's shaft.

tapestry ornamental cloth hanging woven on a loom with silk, gold and silver thread, and characterized by a pictorial design based on preliminary models, called cartoons*. In the early Middle Ages the French town of Arras (from which derives *arazzo*, the Italian word for tapestry) was a major manufacturing centre, but by the 14th and 15th centuries most of the production had shifted to Flanders.

"tarsia" → inlay.

telamon large figure used as a pillar or column to support a structural weight; also called Atlas, from the name of the mythological giant who held up the world on his shoulders.

tetramorphic (Gk. *tetra-*, 'four' + *morphè*, 'shape') a fantastic creature combining the features of man, ox, eagle and lion. The term derives from ancient astrology and is described both in the Book of Ezekiel and in the Apocalypse.

thurible (Gk. *thûr*, 'incense' + *bállo*, 'throw') a censer used for religious ceremonies. In the Catholic church it is a vessel that hangs from three chains and contains a grill on which to burn the incense.

triumphal arch in early Christian churches (called 'basilicas'), the great arch which leads into the apse* and is often mosaicked.

trabeated constructed with posts and lintels.

tympanum (Gk. *túmpanon*, 'membrane') a triangular face enclosed inside the pediment (upper part of a façade) of a temple, door or shrine. It may be decorated with reliefs.

vault a curved, concave ceiling. The 'barrel' (or 'tunnel') vault has a semi-circular shape, while the 'groin' vault, a typical feature of Gothic architecture, is the result of the intersection of two barrel vaults.

volute decorative spiral or coil shape.

women's gallery in early Christian churches, an upper storey reserved for women; usually running along the edges of the aisles and opening on the nave.

Select Bibliography

The bibliography dealing with the Baptistery and the works of art associated with it is indeed very extensive. Here we have listed the major contributions to the subject, with an eye especially to those publications which the reader will easily find in most well-stocked bookshops.

Sources

Giovanni Villani's *Cronica* was published in full in *Croniche di Giovanni, Matteo e Filippo Villani*, Trieste, Sezione letterario-artistica del Lloyd austriaco, 1857-1858; for a selection from this work, see *Cronica, con le continuazioni di Matteo e Filippo*, a cura di G. Aquilecchia, Torino, Einaudi, 1979. Further readings: Lorenzo Ghiberti's *Commentaries* – I *Commentari*, Napoli, Ricciardi, 1947; *I commentarii (Biblioteca Nazionale Centrale di Firenze, II, I, 333)*, Firenze, Giunti, 1998 – and Alessio Baldovinetti's *Memoirs (I Ricordi nuovamente pubblicati e illustrati da G. Poggi*, Firenze 1909). Giorgio Vasari's *Lives of the Artists* was originally published in Florence in two different versions: the 1550 Lorenzo Torrentino edition (see *Le Vite de' più eccellenti architetti, pittori, et scultori italiani, da Cimabue, insino a' tempi nostri*, Torino, Einaudi, 1986) and the 1568 edition by Giunti (see *Le Vite de' più eccellenti pittori scultori et architetti*, Milano, Club del libro, 1962). Both editions were published by Sansoni (Firenze, 1966-1988). For English translations, see *The lives of the artists*, translated with an introduction and notes by J. Conaway Bondanella and P. Bondanella, Oxford-New York, Oxford UP, 1991; *Lives of the artists*, a selection translated by G. Bull, Harmondsworth, Penguin, 1987.

Critical Studies

M. SALMI, *Lezioni di Storia dell'Arte Medievale. Il Battistero di Firenze. Anno accademico 1949-1950*, Roma, Edizioni dell'Ateneo, 1950.

A. DE WITT, *I mosaici del Battistero di Firenze*, Firenze, Cassa di Risparmio di Firenze, 1954-1959, 4 voll.

I.J. HUECK, *Das Programm der Kuppelmosaiken im Florentiner Baptisterium*, Mondorf/Rhein, Krupinski, 1962.

F. ROSSI, *Il San Giovanni, Santa Maria del Fiore, l'Opera del Duomo*, Firenze, Arnaud, 1964.

P. SANPAOLESI-M. BUCCI (edited by), *Duomo e Battistero di Firenze*, Firenze, Sadea-Sansoni, 1966.

L. BECHERUCCI-G.BRUNETTI, *Il Museo dell'Opera del Duomo di Firenze*, Milano-Firenze, Electa, 1969-1970, 2 voll.

R. KRAUTHEIMER, *Ghiberti's Bronze Doors*, Princeton N.J., Princeton UP, 1971.

G. MARCHINI, *Il Battistero e il Duomo di Firenze*, Firenze, Becocci, 1972.

C. PIETRAMELLARA, *Battistero di San Giovanni a Firenze. Rilievo e studio critico*, [rilievo a cura dell'Istituto di restauro dei monumenti], Firenze, Polistampa, 1973.

E.W. ANTHONY, *Early Florentine Architecture and Decoration*, New York, Hacker Art Books, 1975 (orig. ed. Cambridge 1927).

Lorenzo Ghiberti "materia e ragionamenti", catalogo della mostra (Firenze, Museo dell'Accademia e Museo di San Marco, 18 ottobre 1978-31 gennaio 1979), Firenze, Centro Di, 1978.

The Florence Baptistery doors, photos by D. Finn, introduction by K. Clark, commentaries by G. Robinson, New York, Viking Press, 1980.

M. BURRESI, *Andrea, Nino e Tommaso scultori pisani*, con un profilo storico sull'arte pisana del Trecento di A. Caleca, Milano, Electa, 1983.

J. BECK, *Le porte del Battistero di Firenze*, Firenze, Scala, 1985.

A. BUSIGNANI-R. BENCINI, *Le chiese di Firenze. Il Battistero di San Giovanni*, Firenze, Sansoni, 1988.

M. PRETI, *Museo dell'Opera del Duomo di Firenze*, Milano, Electa, 1989.

A. GIUSTI, *Il Battistero di San Giovanni*, Firenze, Messagerie Toscane, 1990.

T. VERDON (edited by), *Dal Battistero al Duomo*, Firenze, Centro Di, 1992 (Alla riscoperta di Piazza del Duomo in Firenze, 1).

C. ACIDINI LUCHINAT, *Il Battistero e il Duomo di Firenze*, Milano, Electa, 1994.

P. DEGL'INNOCENTI, *Le origini del bel San Giovanni: da tempio di Marte a Battistero di Firenze*, presentazione di F. Gurrieri, Firenze, CUSL, 1994.

G. DI CAGNO, *The Cathedral, the Baptistery and the Campanile*, Firenze, Mandragora, 1994.

A. PAOLUCCI (edited by), *Il Battistero di San Giovanni a Firenze*, Modena, Panini, 1994, 2 voll.

D. CARDINI (edited by), *Il bel San Giovanni e Santa Maria del Fiore. Il centro religioso di Firenze dal Tardo Antico al Rinascimento*, presentazione di F. Cardini, Firenze, Le Lettere, 1996.

A. PAOLUCCI, *The origins of Renaissance art: the Baptistry doors, Florence*, translated by F. Pouncey Chiarini, New York, Braziller, 1996.

G. ROCCHI COOPMANS DE YOLDI, (edited by), *Santa Maria del Fiore. Rilievi, documenti, indagini strumentali, interpretazioni: piazza, battistero, campanile*, Firenze, Università degli studi di Firenze, 1996.

A. BICCHI-A. CIANDELLA, *Testimonia Sanctitatis. Le reliquie e i reliquiari del Duomo e del Battistero di Firenze*, Firenze, Mandragora, 1999.

Table of Contents

Printed by Alpilito - Firenze
July 2000